BEHIND THE BLIP

Also by the author

Editor:
Flyposter Frenzy: Posters from the Anticopyright Network
Unnatural

Co-Editor:
README! ASCII Culture and the Revenge of Knowledge

Author:
ATM

BEHIND THE BLIP

ESSAYS ON THE
CULTURE OF SOFTWARE

MATTHEW FULLER

//AUTONOMEDIA

Autonomedia
P.O.B. 568 Williamsburgh Station
Brooklyn, NY 11211-0568 USA
Phone & Fax: 718-963-2603
email: info@autonomedia.org
http://www.autonomedia.org

Book design: Dave Mandl

ISBN 1-57027-139-9

Printed in Canada

For Mandie, Leon, Milo, and Rosa

ACKNOWLEDGEMENTS

"A Means of Mutation" arises from work by the group I/O/D (http://bak.spc.org/iod). Thanks to Simon Pope and Colin Green for several years of it. "Break the Law of Information" is connected to a project run on behalf of the group Mongrel. Thanks to Harwood, Mervin Jarman, Richard Pierre Davis, Matsuko Yokokoji, and all the other participants in Natural Selection. "Long, Dark Phone-In of the Soul" was originally published in *Mute*. Thanks to all the crew there. "Visceral Façades" and "It Looks Like You're Writing a Letter" were first published in *Telepolis*. Thanks to Armin Medosch, then-editor of this website. The work on Microsoft Word was supported by Norwich School of Art and Design. Thanks to Hilary Bedder, Helen Boorman, George MacLennan, and Simon Wilmoth for setting up a research environment sufficiently hands-off to let me get hands on such intractable material. "The Impossibility of Interface" was written during a sabbatical from Middlesex University. Thanks to all staff and students in Media, Culture, and Communications there.

All of the texts in this book have appeared in one shape or another on the mailing list Nettime. Thanks to the moderators and all those who make this such a useful resource. It should also be acknowledged that this work arises from the activity of friends, workmates, readers, users, distributors, copiers, events, discussants: activity that would be endless were it nameable—thanks.

Thanks to the Autonomedia collective and to David Mandl for engineering the book so generously and expertly.

CONTENTS

BEHIND THE BLIP:
SOFTWARE AS CULTURE
(SOME ROUTES INTO "SOFTWARE CRITICISM," MORE WAYS OUT)

SOFTWARE CRITICISM?

There are two questions which I would like to begin with. First, what kind of critical and inventive thinking is required to take the various movements in software forward into those areas which are necessary if software oligopolies are to be undermined? But further, how are we to develop the capacity for unleashing the unexpected upon software and the certainties which form it?

Second, what currents are emerging which demand and incorporate new ways of thinking about software?

One of the ways to think about this problem is to imagine it as a series of articles from a new kind of computer magazine.[1] What would happen if writers about computers expanded their horizons from the usual close focus on benchtests and bit-rates? What would happen if we weren't looking at endless articles detailing the functionality of this or that new version of this or that application? What if we could think a little more broadly—beyond the usual instructional articles describing how to use this filter or that port? What, for instance, would it mean to have a fully fledged "software criticism"?

First, let's look at what already exists. Certainly, we are not short of examples of prior art. In terms of the academy, sociology,

for instance, offers: Jeannette Hofmann's descriptions of the gen-
dering of word processor software and its patterns of use within
work;[2] Paul N. Edwards's history of the development of computer
technologies through the models of science promotable at the
height of the early cold war;[3] Michael R. Curry's formulation of a
technico-aesthetic economy of signification and ownership in geographic information systems;[4] Donald MacKenzie's work on the
political implications of floating-point-unit calculations in the
design of missile guidance systems[5]—the list goes on and extends
to substantial areas in ethnography and anthropology.[6] Material
based around philosophy and literature includes Michael Heim's
Electric Language[7] and the contributions of Friedrich Kittler, despite
his assertions that the object of attention here does not exist.[8] We
can also look to texts which come out of bookshops, but that don't
get libraried up so much: Howard Rheingold's *Tools for Thought*[9]
and J. David Bolter's *Turing's Man,*[10] for instance. This list is certainly short, but it does continue. The creation of imaginary book-
shelves is as good a way of thinking through combinations as the
imaginary museum, and there are three areas in particular which
seem to offer elements recomposable into a more thoroughgoing
strand of thought about and with software.

HUMAN–COMPUTER INTERFACE

Human–Computer Interface (HCI) is obviously one area that
should be turned to. This is, after all, the point at which the machi-
nations of the computer are compelled to make themselves available in one way or another to a user. The way the computer makes
available such use, and the assumptions made about what possible
interactions might develop, are both fundamentally cultural.

Given this, HCI has an unusually narrow understanding of its
scope. Much of the rhetoric is about empowerment and the sover-
eignty of the user, whose "personality" shapes and dialogues with
the machine. It should be asked what model of a persona, what
"human," is engineered by HCI. We should not settle for answers
that stray anywhere near the singalong theme-tune of "empowerment." (Let us not forget that much of the methodology of HCI is
still derived from theories that led B. F. Skinner to assume that he

could train pigeons—in the days before Cruise—to act as primitive guidance systems for missiles.)

It seems clear that the vast majority of research and production in this area remains concerned with imposing functionalist models on all those systems that cohere as the user. Perhaps given software's basis in boolean logic, where every action must be transmogrified into a series of ons and offs held in hundreds of thousands of circuits, this is inevitable at a certain level. Make no mistake, HCI works. It is productive because it belongs to a long line of disciplinary idealisations of the human that nevertheless have the capacity to latch onto flesh. The mainstream of HCI is considered here to be those largely positivist approaches which are represented in standard formulations of the discipline such as the *Handbook of Human–Computer Interaction.*[11] When it comes to arranging the most suitable combination of ergonomics and information-design to ensure that a pilot can drop bombs or stockbrokers can move funds in the most efficient, information-rich, yet graphically and emotionally uncluttered manner, HCI delivers the goods. Reaction times—the number of interactive steps from task identification to task execution—can be measured. The results can be tabulated against variants of the system. The whole can be fine-tuned, pixels shifted, operatives retrained: the loop between stimulus and response tightened into a noose. This is the fatal endpoint of the standard mode of HCI. It empowers users by modelling them, and in doing so effects their disappearance, their incorporation into its models.

There are, of course, many "human-centred" variants on such designs. Yet this kind of naming illustrates its fatal flaw. There is still a model of the human—what constitutes it, how it must be interfaced—being imposed here. Some developments in software design have been made by acknowledging this. Alan Cooper's[12] approach to interface design works, for instance, by establishing a number of stereotypical users of a system. They are imagined as full "characters," users of a system which is reworked, primarily in terms of interface, in order to meet an aggregate of their needs. The deliberate fiction of user identities is made visible at the design stage in order to allow greater insight into the techno-aesthetic composition of the software. A small, useful step would be to make these manufactured identities, but treat them as psycho-social open source.[13]

More broadly, much could be gained by a change in the focus of HCI. In its emphasis on perception, on narrowly applied psychology, it has split the user from any context. One thing that is compelling about software is how it contains models of involvement with processes rather than simply with static elements— think about groupware, or the way in which most previously discrete applications have become part of wider suites of processes, to say nothing about the inherently modular nature of Unix. What would it mean to incorporate an explicitly wider notion of such processes into software—to reinfuse the social, the dynamic, the networks, the political, communality (perhaps even instead of, or as well as, privacy)—into the contained model of the individualised user that HCI has us marked down for?

We can see movements toward this in sociology- and psychology-derived currents within HCI such as Participatory Design. Here, there is a range of collaboration between users and designers that aims to stake out a territory for certain models of what a user becomes interfaced to. Notably, this territory can sometimes even be defined geographically, as in the institutional, corporate, and trade union uptake of this approach in Scandinavia. What these approaches allow is a removal of the more or less negative preconditions of the standard model of HCI that is simply applied to users by experts. The area of Computer Supported Co-operative Work brings some of these elements together, but largely as a way of making them function, of turning them to account.

One tendency that is of interest here is in the proliferation of higher-level languages and authorware. These allow for currents of design that place value on experimentation, rather than adherence to pre-formatted notions of functionality, to invade the conceptual and practical space of the computer. At the same time, capacities for invention do not belong solely to those who most often claim them; the problem of design, of interface, must be set in wider terms.

A key problem here, though, is the danger that a set of questions tend to stabilise out as particular techniques in which something gets solved. Software is a place where many energies and formations meet. At the same time, it constantly slaps up against its limitations, but these are limitations of its own making, formulated by its own terms of composition. Software is always an unsolved problem. We need ways of thinking into and activating this process of becoming, rather than some "kinder" or more "creative" design.

PROGRAMMERS' SELF-ACCOUNTS

Another pre-existing area that offers insights for an understanding of software as culture is the tradition of accounts of their work by programmers. Key texts are "Perl, the First Postmodern Computer Language,"[14] by Larry Wall, and *Close to the Machine*,[15] by Ellen Ullman. Both of these in their own ways document the interrelation of programming with other formations—cultural, social, aesthetic. These are drives that are built into and compose software rather than use it as a neutral tool.

These accounts of programming are somewhat at odds with the idealist tendencies in computing. In the recent film based on Robert Harris's novel *Enigma*, one of the characters makes the claim most succinctly: "With numbers, truth and beauty are the same thing." Such statements are the pop-science version of the attractions of so-called "pure" mathematics. It is also the vision of numbers that most often finds its way to the big screen. (Think also of the film *Pi*, where a cute crazy loner struggles for a glimpse of the numerical meta-reality.) But more crucially, they are a direct route to the cultural backbone of classical idealism. There are harmonious relations between forms of every kind that can be understood through the relations between numbers. The closer they are to achieving purity of form, the more beautiful they become. There is an endpoint to this passage to beauty which is absolute beauty. Access to and understanding of this beauty is allowed only to those souls that are themselves beautiful.

The consequences of such ordering are of course clear, if only in the brutality of their collaboration with and succour for hierarchies of every kind. The kitschier end of this tendency is found, in computing, in accounts such as *The Aesthetics of Computing*.[16] But it is far more violently enhanced by computing when it works to provide an aesthetics of social control. There are far more opportunities offered by constructional and fabulatory approaches. Numbers do not provide big answers, but rather opportunities to explore further manifold and synthetic possibilities—that is to say, they provide access to more figures.

CRITICAL THEORY

Under the aisle-headings Critical, Social, Political, Cultural, Material, Visual, Aesthetic or Blahblah Theory there is a warehouse of tools available, tools which are held back from invading the conceptual domains of software by the myth of its own neutrality as a tool. These rubrics themselves are only really of any use when they are disingenuous, when they don't quite fit. For this reason, there's no option of chewing through the Dewey Decimal System and tabulating them. (The use of the term "theory" is here meant simply as that which develops a model of an approach to the material it works on as it uses it, and with which it shares an equal importance in terms of its production. It therefore acts in relation to other such models at the same time as operating in the field on which it attends. This might be true to some extent of writings on HCI and in programmers' self-accounts, but these are always primarily, rather than equally, concerned in epistemological terms with the accomplishment of an instrumental task.) Here, it is only necessary to make two suggestions, one in terms of scale, the other in terms of activity.

In general, critiques of technologies, particularly media, are made on the basis of a category or class of objects, rather than specific instances of that class.[17] Perhaps the timescale of literary production precludes anything else, but it is also a question of pretensions to timelessness. Why spend time working into a piece of software, when it'll be reversioned in a couple of months? The kind of material that is now gathered to beat students about the heads with as "cyberculture" is generally exemplary in this way. Would it not make more of the gift of your wisdom to the human race to ponder the verities of some enormous category that will combine shelf-longevity and discourse-redeployment potential? It is not that such work is strictly non-empirical, but that in being concerned with offering grand theory-panoramas and generic summations any chance of latching into particularities, particularly those against which such concepts can be tested, disappears under the clouds.

That timescales need also not be determined by corporate release schedules in producing an analysis of software is suggested by Donald Knuth[18] when he proposes a deceptively simple task for computer scientists: Analyse every process that your computer executes in one second. Writing at the end of the eighties, he suggests the number of tasks will be around 250,000. Perhaps this would provide sufficient scope? Timelessness condenses, and the researcher appears years later having annotated an entire second's worth of hundreds of thousands of instructions. Most of the transcript would of course consist of repetitions of instructions carried out on minutely incremental changes in variables. Why not contaminate this simple telling of the story of what goes on inside a computer with its all-too-cultural equivalent? The transcript of the contents of a mind over one day, or of a memory in the transit of a morsel of cake from plate to mouth, provided opportunities for sentences in "fiction" to slide in and out of scale, from layer to layer, in convulsions of sprouting, connecting text. Perhaps the same can also be done at this scale?

At another scale, one of the advantages of the work of Jakob Nielsen, Donald Norman, and others is precisely that they focus in on very specific problems, albeit those of a narrow cast and range of interpretation. Although they tend to deal in a somewhat over-literal application of cybernetic "constraint" rather than the generation of its twin, "freedom," their focus allows them to claim at the very least the rhetorical power of practice. Nit-picking has the capacity to become another mode of the war of the flea. Theorisations of software that are able to operate on the level of a particular version of a program, a particular file structure, protocol, sampling algorithm, colour-scheme, API, Request For Comment, and so on, are necessary. Further, it is essential to understand any such element or event as only one layer or node in a wider set of intersecting and multi-scalar formations. That is to say that, whilst within a particular set of conditions its function might well be to impose stasis upon another element, such an effect cannot always be depended upon. In addition, whilst one might deal with a particular object, it must always be understood not as something static, although it may never change, but to be operating in participial[19] terms.

Such a focus on the unfolding of the particular—with an attention to how they are networked out into further vectors, layers, nodes of classes, instrumentalisations, panics, quick fixes, slow collapses, the sheerly alien fruitfulness of digital abundance, ways in which they can be taken up and made strange, mundane, and beautiful—will at least ensure two things. First, that it busts the locks on the tastefully-interiored prison of stratified interdisciplinarity. It would be a dire fate to end up with a repetition of the infinitely recessive corridor of depleted jargons and zombie conferencing of Film Studies. Second, and in terms of activity, that an engaged process of writing on software might reasonably hope to avoid the fate of much recent cultural theory, that is to say, to step outside of its over-eager subordination to one end of the schematic of information theory: reception.

AVERSION TO THE ELECTRONIC: A HALLMARK OF CONCEPTUALITY?

As an example of where theoretical work presents us with an opportunity to go further, I want to run through a particular example.

In their book *What Is Philosophy?*,[20] Gilles Deleuze and Félix Guattari present a back-to-basics manifesto. Philosophy has become the domain of men whose occupation is the construction of vast hulks of verbiage—immense dark ships with their single-minded captains, vessels constructed of words, unable, unwilling even to communicate amongst themselves and which, as a result, pass each other by in the night.

The book is at once a rescue of philosophy from its status as doomed élite subculture staffed by the populations of the soon-to-be closed ghost departments of the universities of Europe, and also a restatement of the primary task of philosophy: the invention of concepts. In order to state their case for this, they need to clear the decks of other ways in which the word *concept* is used. One of the problems they see facing their use of the term is that

> in successive challenges, philosophy faced increasingly insolent and calamitous rivals that Plato himself would have never imagined in his most comic moments. Finally the most shameful moment came when computer science, marketing, design, and advertising, all the disciplines of communication, seized hold of the word *concept* itself and said: "This is our concern, we are the creative ones, we are the ideas men! We are the friends of the concept, we put it in our computers."[21]

As is well known, their work is in many ways an immense, vibrant resource. However, it appears that there is a particular blockage, more so perhaps in the work of Deleuze than of Guattari,[22] when it comes to a useable theorisation of media. There is a tendency here which is typical, not just of their work, but of much theoretical work throughout the twentieth century. Whilst some media systems, such as books, music, painting, film, etc., are entered into with a profound spirit of exploration and invention, those that are electronic are treated as being fundamentally suspicious.

As a result, when they do touch on electronic media, their work jumps into and out of various similarly short and undifferentiated takes. In short, electronic media do participate in "conceptuality." The conceptual personae that Deleuze and Guattari so suggestively propose in *What Is Philosophy?* can be read as a proposal for an understanding of software as a form of digital subjectivity—that software constructs sensoriums, that each piece of software constructs ways of seeing, knowing, and doing in the world that at once contain a model of that part of the world it ostensibly pertains to and that also shape it every time it is used.

(This is what Kathy Acker is pointing to when the stolen software in *Empire of the Senseless* appears as a live, severed head.) Further, that each software element commonly interprets and remodulates what is understood to be the same, or a similar, process. For instance, the various takes on writing (plain text-editing, word processing, markup, and so on) presented by editors such as BBEdit, vi, Microsoft Word, LaTeX, etc.[23]

Whilst this domain of non-philosophical concepts is characterised as shameless and inane, it is unusual to find these materialists drawing such a concrete boundary beyond which creation and an experimental politics cannot exist. My impression, though, is that this is the result of a confusion, which can be read through conflicting tendencies in Deleuze and Guattari's own work. These should be read as pointers to problematics which certainly exist in the production of a theory of software. They are warnings, but ones that cannot be said to provide absolute stoppage to the inventive powers that lie in this area.

The tension between the approaches combined in their writings is clear. In terms of the wider field of electronic media, it is perhaps best seen in the way in which TV is described as a force that bridges the gap between the Althusserian models of repression and ideology, by offering simultaneous subjection and enslavement. That is, that viewers recognise themselves as the subject of interpolation of the television, but at the same time in a state of cybernetic submission to its sequence of switches, flashes of light, and bursts of input.[24]

Anyone who has watched CNN during the war over the monopoly on terror will know the moralistic slavery that is already presupposed of its audience by these broadcasters, the "we" that is called to order by its clatter of statements and opinions. What Deleuze and Guattari describe is clearly a tendency, an attractor, within media systems, but cannot be said to be a compelling description. Instead such theoretical positions need to be opened up.

Whilst they are almost useless in their direct characterisations of electronic media, the tools to do some of this opening up can of course be found in the same books. This is a characteristic of what

Robert Cooper calls their capacity to produce "generic,"[25] mobile concepts. In their writings on war machines—assemblages at any scale and of any type that attack or break free of total positioning systems—and their relationships to state formations, they note that

> (doubtless) the State apparatus tends to bring uniformity to the regimes, by disciplining its armies, by making work a fundamental unit, in other words, by imposing its own traits. But it is not impossible for weapons and tools, if they are taken up by new assemblages of metamorphosis, to enter other relations of alliance.[26]

Computers must be understood already as assemblages. In his *Lectures on Computation,* Richard Feynman notes research that specifies thirteen levels to an operating system. "This goes from level 1, that of electronic circuitry—registers, gates, buses—to number 13, the Operating System Shell, which manipulates the user programming environment. By a hierarchical compounding of instructions, basic transfers of 1's and 0's on level one are transformed, by the time we get to thirteen, into commands to land aircraft in a simulation or check whether a forty-digit number is prime."[27] Since the time of his writing, 1984, many more "levels" have become involved: The various protocols of interface, licensing, network, the ways in which computation has been coded and styled for various markets, are only a few examples. What is contended here is that any one of these levels provides an opportunity for critique, but more importantly for forms of theorisation and practice that break free of any preformatted uniformity. Since it is what they are further assembled with that determines their metamorphosis, it is the task of such practical and theoretical work to open these layers up to the opportunity of further assemblage.

Curiously, this is precisely the lesson that Deleuze and Guattari draw from another form of electronic media, the synthesiser. What is the "thought synthesiser"[28] that they suggest? By assembling modules, source elements, and elements for treating concepts (oscillators, generators, and transformers), by arranging microintervals, the synthesiser makes conceptualisable the philosophical process, the production of that process itself, and puts us

in contact with other elements of matter. In this machine composed by its materiality and force, thought travels, becomes
mobile, synthesises.

Why, in their reading of the synthesiser, is there no dismay at
humans merely providing a relay system between the variable
actuations of a circuit board? It is certainly to pay attention to the
wider assemblages which they form and are formed by. Because to
describe the synthesiser as terminally as they do the TV would be
to give up, to stop making a machine in the machine.

PRODUCTION

Instead of criticism, then—software criticism per se—what I want
to suggest is that we pay attention to some practices within software production that emerge with and through thought out of
whack with its simple reproduction.

Criticism proper, the self-abrogated privilege of judgement, is
always predicated on finding itself absent from what it critiques.
This true thought of the outside is that which can find no point of
connection with what it surveys—except, that is, in pleasure in the
announcement of its absolute corruption. Is anyone capable of
such magnificent isolation? And this is why it is necessary to present some models of software production that contain engines for its
theorisation. These are models that have arisen from work done
over the last few years by a number of groups. No special claim is
made that they exhaust any set of possibilities, nor that any of
these models excludes characteristics given under another heading;
they simply form notes on work going on.

CRITICAL SOFTWARE

One of the ways in which the currents described here first became
manifest is in the creation of pieces of software designed explicitly
to pull the rug from underneath normalised understandings of software. In 1957 Roland Barthes prefaced *Mythologies,* his collection
of essays on the common-sensical mores of then-contemporary
French bourgeois life, with the phrase, "Sarcasm is the condition of
truth."[29] Nowadays there is no need to dispute sarcasm's unique

access to enlightenment. What is redundant now is any condition-ality. Sarcasm *is* truth. Critical software is a voyage into that truth by means of its own devices.

What are the ways in which critical software operates? There are two key modes. First, by using the evidence presented by nor-malised software to construct an arrangement of the objects, pro-tocols, statements, dynamics, and sequences of interaction that allow its conditions of truth to become manifest. This is the mode of operation of the installation "A Song for Occupations," which simply maps out the entire interface of Microsoft Word to reveal the blue-grey labyrinth in which writing is so happily lost. Richard Wright's CD-ROM *Hello World* takes a similar tack in making a comparative analysis of the interfaces and data structures—and consequent ways of knowing, seeing, and doing—of various video-editing and -effects packages such as Quantel, After Effects, and Flame.

The second way in which Critical Software may be said to exist is in the various instances of software that runs just like a normal application, but has been fundamentally twisted to reveal the underlying construction of the user, the way the program treats data, and the transduction and coding processes of the interface. Much of this work has been achieved in terms of games. Jodi's work on Wolfenstein and Quake is paradigmatic here, but there is a whole run of work, using mod files and patches, that can be seen in this light.[30] Additionally, there is a strand of work that has been cracked and messed with, by means of programs such as ResEdit, in order to gain access to its kernel of truth. The interfaces of stan-dard software packages are rewritten.[31] Perhaps some of the actions defacing websites can also be said to belong to this current.[32] What this work does is make apparent the processes of normalisation operating at many scales within software—the ways in which, for instance, millions of separate writing acts are dedifferentiated by the various layers of a word processing program. By acting within it in a way that is both investigative and emetic, it points towards a move beyond the boundaries observed in simple institutional cri-tique, towards other modes of creation. Not only that, but it per-forms the necessary task of allowing a negativistic maggot to remain in all the golden apples of the two currents that follow, lest they be mistaken for a simply positive contribution to the empire of happiness.

SOCIAL SOFTWARE

Social software can provisionally be said to have two strands. Primarily it is software built by and for those of us locked out of the narrowly engineered subjectivity of mainstream software. It is software which asks itself what kind of currents, what kinds of machine, numerical, social, and other dynamics, it feeds in and out of, and what others can be brought into being.

The second strand is related to this. It is software that is directly born, changed, and developed as the result of an ongoing sociability between users and programmers in which demands are made on the practices of coding that exceed their easy fit into standardised social relations

In most cases, these two threads interweave. It is how they do so, how their multiple elements are brought into communication and influence, that determines their level of success.

I would like to suggest that Free Software can be usefully understood to work in these terms. It is a socio-technical pact between users of certain forms of license, language, and environment. The various forms of free or open-source software are developed as part of the various rhythms of life of software production. In addition, new social machines are invented to spawn the code, to diffuse and manage its development.

The pace and style of life in these forms of software development and diffusion can be understood to form their internal culture. For many, this is a functional utopia for coders, brought about by digital abundance. Much could be said about the way in which open-source code interrelates with the world of work—how class libraries function as a form of solidarity between programmers in minimising labour-time, but also how technical obscurantism is necessitated in order to maintain the caste privilege.

Thus, the second thread in this proposed conception of social software is partially met by the various strands of the open source movement. The ongoing sociability between users and programmers is there precisely because the users and programmers are one and the same. As is commonly acknowledged, this has provided the motivating force for the first stages of this movement. Why is Apache the best web server software? Because it is written by those who know these systems best.

But this has also formed a blockage to wider uptake of such systems. Free software is too internalist. The relation between its users and its developers is so isomorphic that there is extreme difficulty in breaking out of that productive but constricted circle. One way out of this is seen as finding ways in which free software can bring itself into communication with users who are not also its primary developers. This is crucial, but it is how it is done, and how it weaves this connection with the first thread of social software, that will determine its success. New imaginal and communicative capacities to enter into relations of becoming—of machine, technical, aesthetic, and social dynamics—are required. And it is here that free software now faces its biggest problem.

Free software taps into the dynamics of mutual aid, of shared resources, code conservation, and plagiarism, to get itself made. Now it needs to begin to set technico-aesthetic agendas which open and set flying the ways of sensing, knowing, and doing built into proprietary software. Death to bludgeoning pseudo-rationalism, and the feature-breeding world as office! Supposedly free software projects such as K Office are fundamentally flawed. They may have freedom in the sense of free speech, but this speech is not the result of free thought. Their composition is determined by a submissive relation to the standards set by Microsoft. This is a deliberate abdication of the imagination in dealing with the culture and structuration of all the kinds of work that take place in offices, a failure to take up the possibility of the reinvention of writing that digital technology offers.

In order to escape the impasse of open-source internalism, the developers of this mode of free software have attempted to connect to other kinds of users. But the users they are attempting to recruit

are precisely those formed and normalised by proprietary software. (By this I mean not the actual users of the software, but the
models of them that are put into place by that software—and which
it is therefore unable to distinguish and learn from.)

The mobilisation of free software by corporations is not my
theme here, although what is perhaps most crucial but invisible in
software—the model of life, the figuration of a user determined by
these organisations—has yet to prove anything other than fundamentally entropic to innovation in these areas. The challenge to
free software is that although it has massified its user base to some
extent it faces the danger, not yet the actuality, of becoming conceptually stalled. This kind of reinvention might well be taken up
by others.

One of the ways in which this is being done is via a mobilisation of elements in the first thread of social software. How far can
the thinking about free software be opened by viewing itself as part
of this wider tendency? One easy answer is that it allows the possibility of finding and communicating with users other than those
modelled by pre-existing proprietary software. If the second thread
of social software is born out of extended negotiation between
users and developers, even to the extent that the difference
between them is blurred, what are the ways we can ensure that
that communication does not result in a closing back in on itself
into another isomorphic circle? Primarily by insisting on the
inevitable disequilibrium of relations between the user and the
programmer. This is a political fact which cannot be avoided.
Despite the fact that free software makes public the labour which
is repressed from visibility under proprietary software, it is still the
case that whoever is "closest to the machine" owns the space of
possibilities which the relations have been established to explore.[33]

How can this disequilibrium be tipped over into a kind of
movement other than that of absolute polar attraction by the
"expert"? The first thread of social software offers us some routes
into this problem. The answer is, inevitably, more careful work,
more attention, more openness to difficulty and connection. We
can only generate social software in its full sense through fundamental research into the machine, numerical, social, and other

dynamics that software feeds in and out of. However, these systems need to be understood in a sense expanded from that which software currently allows itself to know. The problem is not in recognising other forms of "expertise" and finding ways of accessing them. (We might consider as an opposite tendency the example of an artists' collective developing a city-mapping initiative in which they are only able to communicate with other "professionals" such as architects, critics, and theorists. Such is the stratified poverty of inter-disciplinarity.) There is a far more important need to recognise and find ways of coming into alliance with forms of intelligence that are excluded from the depleted culture of experts.

One of these, I would like to argue, is a poetics of connection.

There are ways in which technologies are taken over in ways that surpass product specifications. One of the most recent and notable examples is the use of the SMS protocol on GSM mobile phones. To manufacturers and network operators this cranky little texting facility was seen as a novelty, a little nothing, a gimmick. Instead, it has taken off and becomes what is well known today.

For many ostensibly radical theorisations of technology and media this is a problem. Perhaps we will always return here to a base–superstructure model: That is, property relations ultimately determine use. Under this rubric, there are two problem with texting, and with mobiles in general. First, the networks are centralised, running on a spoke-to-hub topology. They are owned by a multinational oligopoly. Second, their standards are not open: They cannot be accessed, improved upon, or reinvented except in compliance with the needs of these companies. This theory is able to account for why there has been no substantially innovative work by artists using mobile phones alone—there is no way of messing with the architecture. (It has to be collaged with other media systems in order to tease out new possibilities.[34]) And for this reason it is of fundamental use.

What it cannot account for is the way that this technology has been overrun and conceptually, if not infrastructurally, reinvented by hordes of what are seen as rather insignificant non-experts: teenagers, illegal workers, gossip-mongers, and so on. All of these subsist and thrive on their powers of connection, of existing in a dimension of relationality rather than of territoriality. It is in their capacity to generate a poetics of this connection that they have reinvented this technology. (This is now a commonplace, of course, but only in retrospect. And as Sadie Plant notes, it was not even recognised as a possibility by those charitably concerned with widening access to networks like the internet.[35])

Such a dynamic has also formed the basis for the development of a piece of software, Mongrel's Linker.[36] This program is described more fully elsewhere, but it is essentially a small application that allows the fast authoring of multimedia collages. The software was developed by Mongrel to meet its needs for applications that can be introduced and used within a day or two. The functionality—when compared with the software used to create it, Macromedia Director—is massively stripped down. Instead of the interface being the usual grey windowed explosion of digital abundance, you get very little. The processing is shifted to the user. It relies on people's ability to generate narrative, political, melancholy, rhythmic, scattershot associations. It relies on the simple function of doing exactly what the name says it does—linking things. Here, the poetics of connection forms a techno-aesthetic and existential *a priori* to the construction of a piece of software.

This is a piece of software that has built itself up on learning from and through what occurs unofficially, the ways in which people, networks, drives, and languages coalesce to circumvent, parasitise, or overturn what codes, produces, and regulates them. Such an activity should not be understood as safely giving vent to an essential human need. It is pathological as much as anything else. But it is in paying attention to the way these dynamics work in particular instances, in acknowledging the intelligence built into them, that the potential for another form of software comes into view.

Poetics of connection is only one such dynamic. There are many others that could be worked into. The concept of social software, too, provides only something small, a little nothing. But with its two strands, in its necessarily unbalanced and mobile state, it provides another motor for creation, of the social as well as of software.

SPECULATIVE SOFTWARE

The best fiction is always also attempting to deal with the crisis of written language, in the way that it asks itself about the legacy built into text as the result of its birth in the keeping of records, in the establishment of laws, in assembling and managing tables of debt and credit. It does this perpetually, at the same time as reinventing and expanding upon the capacity of language to create new things. Speculative software fulfills something of a similar function for digital cultures. In Ellen Ullman's *Close to the Machine,* she states:

> I'd like to think that computers are neutral, a tool like any other, a hammer that can build a house or smash a skull. But there is something in the system itself, in the formal logic of programs and data, that recreates the world in its own image . . . We place this small projection of ourselves all around us, and we make ourselves reliant on it. To keep information, buy gas, save money, write a letter . . . We conform to the range of motion the system allows. We must be more orderly, more logical. Answer the question Yes or No, OK or Cancel . . . Then, slowly, we incorporate the whole notion of systems: We'll link registration data to surveillance,[37] to contract compliance . . . Finally, we arrive at a tautology: The data prove the need for more data! We think we are creating the system, but the system is also creating us. We build the system, we live in its midst, and we are changed.[38]

Ullman's book is the best account of the lived experience of programming that I've read, but I'm not quite sure who this "we" is. Perhaps it's the same "we" that always turns up when a voiceover speaks slowly over a heavy-concept TV documentary. There are pictures of traffic jams, mobile-phone users, nuclear power plants, cubicled workplaces, and ATMs, probably filmed in black and white, portentousness filters set to stun. The "we" is the "we" as in a tremulous, "What have we done to ourselves?" The "we" is an attempt to universalise rather than identify more precisely definable, albeit massively distributed and hierarchised, sets of conflictual, imaginal, and collaborative relations.

Elsewhere, speculative software has been suggested as being software that explores the potentiality of all possible programming. It creates transversal connections between data, machines, and networks. Software whose work is partly to reflexively investigate itself as software. Software as science fiction, as mutant epistemology.

Speculative software can be understood as opening up a space for the reinvention of software by its own means. That is to say that when, as Ullman suggests, the computer has "its own place where the systems and the logic take over,"[39] this is a place that can be explored, mapped, and messed with by a skewed application of those very same means.

In *Close to the Machine*, the narrator worries about a new payroll system that she's just been hired to work on:

> I'll wonder what I'm doing helping the IRS collect taxes. It will bother me that so many entities—employer, software company, bank, IRS—know so much about the simple act of someone getting paid for labour delivered. I'll think about the strange path of a paycheque direct-deposit, how it goes from employer to bank, company to company, while the person being paid is just a blip, the recipient's account a temporary way-station . . .[40]

Each of these entities—employer, software company, bank, IRS, employee—is composed by myriad interacting and agonistic relations. These blips, these events in software, these processes and regimes that data is subject to and manufactured by, provide flashpoints at which these interrelations, collaborations, and conflicts can be picked out and analysed for their valences of power, for their manifold capacities of control and production, disturbance and invention. It is the assertion of speculative software that the enormous spread of economies, systems of representation, of distribution, hiding, showing, and influence as they mesh with other systems of circulation, of life, ecology, resources—themselves

always both escaping and compelling electronic and digital manifestation—can be intercepted, mapped, and reconfigured precisely
by means of these blips.

What are these blips? They are interpretative and reductive
operations carried out on lived processes. They are the statistical
residues of dynamics of association, escape, misery, acquiescence,
and delight. They are not merely signifiers of an event, but integral
parts of it. The figures in a bank balance, the links appearing in a
web browser, are concrete arrangements, formations that determine relative degrees of potential movement within a specified
level of analysis or use of a system. They have an implicit politics.
Their aesthetics can be described as the result of the range of their
potential combinatorial or isolatory capacity and its allowance of
capture, invention, interrogation, or flight, the rhythms of peace or
of compulsion that they put into place.

There are certain ways in which one is supposed to experience
these blips. They are intended to mean that you are precisely broke
at this time of the week, or that there are so many or no related
web sites outside of the one you are currently viewing. Such statements, of course, are dependent on particular arrangements by
which they can be made. Your wage statement is the cryptic blip
that instantiates the enormous machine of class relations. A list of
links is the result of a particular culture of association amongst a
certain range of types of site, of which the site you are viewing is
one instance.

These instances, these blips, are all manifest digitally. They can
be picked out, mapped, arranged, examined, and placed in comparison with each other. Their modes of emergence and combination can be ascertained along with their conditions of repetition
and change. The capacity of computers to perform these operations
is what provides the fuel for speculative software—that is, software
which refuses to believe the simple, innocent stories that accompany the appearance of these blips. Software that skews, misreads,
and takes them for a little walk, but that not only reinterprets but
leaves an invention of blips in its wake.

It is this capacity for invention and reinvention that is characteristic of digital abundance more generally, however little it is

taken up. What characterises speculative work in software is, first, the ability to operate reflexively upon itself and the condition of being software—to go where it is not supposed to go, to look behind the blip; to make visible the dynamics, structures, regimes, and drives of each of the little events which it connects to. Second, it is to subject these blips and what shapes and produces them to unnatural forms of connection between themselves. To make the ready ordering of data, categories, and subjects spasm out of control. Third, it is to subject the consequences of these first two stages to the havoc of invention.

NOTES

1. Pit Schultz made this suggestion as part of the preparatory work on the Software as Culture thread for Wizards of OS 2: Open Cultures and Free Knowledge, Berlin, October 2001. A version of this text was first prepared for that conference. Further information at: http://www.wizards-of-os.org/

2. Jeannette Hofmann, "Writers, Texts, and Writing Acts: Gendered User Images in Word Processing Software," in Donald MacKenzie and Judy Wacjman, eds., *The Social Shaping of Technology*, second edition (Buckingham: Open University Press, 1999), pp. 222–243.

3. Paul N. Edwards, *The Closed World: Computers and the Politics of Discourse in Cold War America* (Cambridge, MA: MIT Press, 1996).

4. Michael R. Curry, *Digital Places: Living with Geographical Information Systems* (London: Routledge, 1998).

5. Don Mackenzie, *Inventing Accuracy: A Historical Sociology of Nuclear Missile Guidance* (Cambridge, MA: MIT Press, 1990), and *Knowing Machines: Essays on Technical Change* (Cambridge, MA: MIT Press, 1996).

6. See, for instance, the work of Susan Leigh Star and others in *Cultures of Computing* (Oxford, Blackwell, 1995).

7. Michael Heim, *Electric Language: A Philosophical Study of Word Processing* (New Haven: Yale University Press, 1987).

8. Friedrich A. Kittler, *Literature, Media, Information Systems,* ed. John Johnstone, trans. various (Amsterdam: G&B Arts International, 1997).

9. An HTML version of the first edition of *Tools for Thought* is at: http://www.rheingold.com/texts/tft/

10. J. David Bolter, *Turing's Man: Western Culture in the Computer Age* (London: Penguin, 1986).

11. Martin Helander, Thomas Landauer, Prasad Prabhu, *Handbook of Human–Computer Interaction* (Oxford: Elsevier, 1997).

12. Alan Cooper, *The Inmates Are Running the Asylum* (Indianapolis: Sams Publishing, 1999). Cooper's approach is a particularly developed formulation of a range of procedures current in HCI's relation to users. A related set of processes for working through variable possibilities in interface and functionality is described, for instance, by Joy Mountford in "Tools and Techniques for Creative Design" in Brenda Laurel, ed., *The Art of Human Computer Interface Design* (Reading, Massachussetts: Addison Wesley, 1990) pp.17–30.

13. Of course, something of the sort is often done in product marketing, where potential customers are assumed to be able to identify with a range of typed user personalities. Phone companies use such approaches to sell tariffs and handsets. Such overt user-formatting is always responded to with the tactics of double-consciousness.

14. At http://www.wall.com/larry/

15. Ellen Ullman, *Close to the Machine* (San Francisco: City Lights, 1997).

16. David Gelerntner, *The Aesthetics of Computing* (London: Phoenix, 1998).

17. Of course, there are plenty of exceptions to this self-generalising statement. One of those that shows a way in which attention to the specificity of a particular technology is rewarded with great clarity is Bruno Latour, "The Berlin Key, or How to Do Words with Things," in P. M. Graves-Brown, ed., *Matter, Materiality and Modern Culture* (London: Routledge, 2000.) Latour's work here is

derived from a current of work, Actor-Network Theory (ANT), which, despite being specifically located in sociology, may well be of substantial use in developing a productive conceptualisation of software. A useful summary of the history of ANT can be found in the first couple of chapters of Mike Michael, *Reconnecting Culture, Technology and Nature: From Society to Heterogeneity* (London: Routledge, 2000).

18. Donald Knuth, "Theory and Practice," address to 11th World Computer Congress, San Francisco, 28 August 1989; archived as a TeX file at http://www-cs-faculty.stanford.edu/~knuth/preprints.html

Such an analysis might provide an insight into how CPU cycle allocation is made on the basis of hierarchies of tasks, which would inevitably contain models of the user. For a useful take on a related problem, see Harwood's "A Manifesto for Useless Art" at http://www.scotoma.org/

19. Elaine Scarry usefully introduces this term. Derived from grammar, it simply means a word that is both a verb and a noun, a thing and a motion. *Resisting Representation* (Oxford University Press, 1994).

20. Gilles Deleuze and Félix Guattari, *What Is Philosophy?*, trans. Hugh Tomlinson and Graham Burchill (London: Verso, 1994).

21. Ibid., p.10.

22. What can be seen as the beginnings of a useful theorisation of electronic media can be seen most clearly in Guattari's "Regimes, Pathways, Subjects," in Gary Genosko, ed., *The Guattari Reader* (Oxford: Blackwell, 1996), and also in Jonathan Crary and Stanford Kwinter, eds., *Incorporations* (New York: Zone, 1992).

The other text in which Guattari makes a real start on such work (but cannot of course be said to have this simply as his focus) is the chapter "Machinic Heterogenesis" in *Chaosmosis: An Ethico-Aesthetic Paradigm* (Sydney: Power Publications, 1995, p. 97).

Elsewhere, in this and other texts, Guattari simply makes passing references to themes close to the ideas of collective intelligence developed by Pierre Lévy, but also invests in the hope of reinventing a new kind of orality through machines (for instance, in

Nicholas Zurbrugg, *Postmodernism and Ethical Abdication,* and Genosko, op. cit., p. 115). Such technology has so far resulted in applications requiring very narrow sets of vocabulary, such as automatic telephone-answering or control of subsidiary dashboard functions in cars, but is of immense interest in terms of its potential to, for instance, reorganize language around archivable orality. (If full voice-recognition is developed, what are the implications for text? All linguistic data could be stored, searched, and cross-referenced as spoken word, with a potentially enormous effect on the way in which forms of speech, text, are currently valued, used, and ordered into hierarchies.)

The scope of the present essay is not a comprehensive philological examination of figurations of the electronic in Deleuze and Guattari, but it might be useful to point towards the material on music and synthesizers compiled by Richard Pinhas at Web Deleuze (http://www.webdeleuze.com/), and also their use of an information-theory model adapted from Rosenstiehl and Petitot to discuss technologies of social control in the "Rhizome" section of *A Thousand Plateaus,* op cit.

23. Thanks to Florian Cramer for a demonstration of vi which brought this sharply into focus. See also, "It Looks Like You're Writing a Letter: Microsoft Word" in this volume.

24. "For example, one is subjected to TV insofar as one uses and consumes it, in the very particular situation of a subject of the statement that more or less mistakes itself for a subject of enunciation ('You, dear television viewers, who make TV what it is . . . '); the technical machine is the medium between two subjects. But one is enslaved by TV as a human machine insofar as television viewers are no longer consumers or users, not even subjects who supposedly 'make' it, but intrinsic component pieces, 'input' and 'output,' feedback or recurrences that are no longer connected to the machine in such a way as to produce or use it. In machinic enslavement, there is nothing but transformations and exchanges of information, some of which are mechanical, others human.' (*A Thousand Plateaus,* p. 458). See also the brief section "If Literature Dies It Will Be Murder" in the interview "Mediators," included in Gilles Deleuze, *Negotiations,* trans. Martin Joughin (New York:

Columbia University Press, 1995), and the perceptive account of the way in which TV formats such as chat shows reduce thought, writing, and dialogue to a series of "positions" in Gilles Deleuze and Claire Parnet, *Dialogues,* trans. Hugh Tomlinson and Barbara Habberjam (London: Continuum, 2002).

25. Robert Cooper, "Assemblage Notes," in Robert C. H. Chia, ed., *Organised Worlds: Explorations in Technology and Organization with Robert Cooper* (London: Routledge, 1998) pp. 108–330.

26. Gilles Deleuze and Félix Guattari, *A Thousand Plateaus,* p. 402.

27. Richard P. Feynman, *Feynman Lectures on Computation,* Anthony J. G. Hey and Robert W. Allen, eds. (London: Penguin, 1996), p. 4. (The article he cites is P. J. Denning & R. L. Brown, "Operating Systems," *Scientific American,* September 1984, p. 96.)

28. Gilles Deleuze and Félix Guattari, *A Thousand Plateaus,* p. 343.

29. Roland Barthes, *Mythologies* (London: Paladin, 1973).

30. A program for the Mac through which the look of an interface, the text of dialogue boxes, and other more intricate resource allocations can be manipulated. An example of this mode might be Heritage Gold, a reversioning of Photoshop 1.0. A useful site on ResEdit is http://www.machacks.com/

31. Two sites monitoring and documenting this form of activity are: http://www.attrition.org and http://www.alldas.de

32. See for instance, the TextFM project to link users of SMS with a means of generating instant audio broadcast via radio: http://www.scotoma.org/TextFM/

33. In another context, the workplace, this "closeness" is meshed into a different set of inter-relations. The degree to which programmers have control over the rate and way in which they work, the way in which they define what is "possible," and the ways in which it might be achieved has of course been one of the key guarantees of their value as labour. Software production management techniques are developed precisely to counter and close down and rationalise such processes.

34. It is also clear that speculative uses of phones were being made by hackers and phreaks as soon as any new technologies or

routes into them became available, and for as long as they've existed in any form. How hacking can be understood to operate as a technico-aesthetic and perceptual activity with important consequences for the themes of this essay is developed amongst other places in Cornelia Sollfrank's Liquid Hacking http://www.obn.org/ LHL/concepte.html and *Hacks,* a documentary by Christine Bader (1997). Info on this film at: http://www.choiproductions.com/

35. Sadie Plant, "On the Phone," Motorola, 2002.

36. The Mongrel web site is at: http://www.mongrelx.org/. Linker is available to download at: http://www.linker.org.uk/. A recent internet-based development of this software, called Nine, maintains its original features, but makes the code and the process of using it more available and open to development. To use or view Nine, check http://9.waag.org/.

A consideration of social software might also be made in relation to Piloot, a custom form of groupware whose development was led at the Society for Old and New Media, Amsterdam:j52

http://www.waag.org/

Another application that might well be understood on these terms is the essential, constantly updated database of reusable software serial numbers, Serial Box, and the program that it replaced, Surfer's Serials.

Perhaps there is something in that these pieces of software are focused only on combining a small set of functions and processes rather than acting as a metacultural factory typical of the large-scale applications. By being clear—or attempting to be so—about what they do, they can be perceived to a greater depth. There is no pretence to be anything but simple mechanisms, with a particular slant. It is perhaps this which allows their ready use or discarding.

37. Note, the specific forms of surveillance Ullman is referring to are workplace systems where logging-on prompts keystroke-counting, recording of web sites visited, etc. This form of worker surveillance forms an inverse of the kind of study that Knuth suggests.

38. Ullman, p. 89.

39. Ullman, p. 188.

40. Ullman, p. 188.

VISCERAL FAÇADES
TAKING MATTA-CLARK'S CROWBAR
TO SOFTWARE

Architecture was the first art of measurement of time and space. Ancient megalithic structures such as Stonehenge are the ancestors of the machines this text was written and set on. Whereas computers build up from the scale of electrons rather than that of giant lumps of stone, and the tasks they complete are abstract and changeable rather than specific and singular, both computers and architecture remain physical instantiations of abstract logic into which energy is fed in order to produce results to one or more of a range of potential calculations embodied in their structure.

Nowadays, as films like *Die Hard* and novels like *Gridlocked* are so keen to show us, buildings and telecommunications are profoundly interrelated. As architecture is caught up in the mesh of the apparent "immaterial," of security and communications systems, of gating and processing (think of an airport), its connection to its originary development as geometry realised in synthetic space becomes ever more apparent. The proliferation of special effects that work on consciousness of time and distance and the perception of the environment—in a context where maximum stratification combines in the same device with maximum fluidity—is presented as an abrupt break with an older style of architecture wherein power can be deciphered by the maximum possession of space.

In the short story "Tangents,"[1] science fiction writer Greg Bear introduces four-dimensional beings into a three-dimensional shape, something that he likens to looking at fish through the corner of an aquarium. The shape that these fourth-dimensional beings appear in is a normal, two-storey house. The house is gradually, neatly swiss-cheesed by a series of cones, columns, and spheres as the dimensions intersect.

This might be the kind of effect you'd worry about if you'd invited Gordon Matta-Clark around to your home. An artist who trained as an architect, Matta-Clark was born in New York City in March 1943 and died in 1978. His most prolific period, between 1971 and 1976, occurred within a rich context of experimental and anti-commercial operations in both art and architecture (although certainly within the fields recognised as corresponding to architectural history, much of this work remained on a theoretical and propositional basis). Matta-Clark carried out his investigations of architecture and space through performance, drawing, sculpture, photography, video, film, and material interventions known as "cuttings."

One action carried out in 1974, documented in the short film *Splitting,* involved taking a simple detached wooden house in Englewood, a New York State dormitory town, and bisecting it. The house, already slated for demolition, is cut exactly in two, from the roof down the walls and through the floors to the raised foundation of building blocks. In the film, a shard of sunlight streams through the split, effacing the wall, energising the new structure. The next stage is to take the rear half of the house and, supporting it on jacks, gradually knock away the upper surface of the foundation at an angle of five degrees. The back of the house is then tilted away from the other half of the structure back onto the now-sloping foundation. Throughout the film, Matta-Clark can be seen working away at the building, a scrawny longhair in jeans and boots doing with a simple toolkit the serious structural readjustment that only the most deranged of do-it-yourselfers can dream about.

Another short film, *Conical Intersect,* made in 1975, documents an intervention which is even more reminiscent of the transdimensional interference of "Tangents." Made during the Paris

Biennial in the area of Les Halles, tellingly close to the construction of the Centre Georges Pompidou—a politically inspired scheme reminiscent of that other *artiste démolisseur,* Baron Haussmann—the cut probes into two adjoining seventeenth-century "mansions." Appearing from the outside as a series of receding circles, the cut punctures the building at the fourth storey and moves upwards towards the sky. When the outer wall goes through, the film shows the grimy trio working on the hole perform a brief can-can on a soon-to-be-demolished section of floor.

In a 1976 film, *Substrait (Underground Dailies),* Matta-Clark explored and documented some of the underground of New York City. Grand Central Station, Thirteenth Street, and the Croton Aqueduct are filmed to show the variety and complexity of the hidden spaces and tunnels in the metropolitan area. Somewhat reminiscent of the exquisitely dull documentaries made by the Canadian National Film Board in the same period, this film develops an intimate concern with the material qualities of the structures under investigation, and perhaps provides for the New York sewage system a precursor to the geek art of the internet. It is possible to imagine a recording of its travels through the nets made by a software worm, being of remarkable similarity.

Some of Matta-Clark's work could only have been produced by someone deeply familiar with the strange reality of realty. In *Reality Properties: Fake Estates,* he bought up fifteen minuscule sections of land that had been left over in property deals, or that teetered just off the edges of architectural plans drawn slightly out-of-whack: a foot-wide strip down somebody's driveway, a square-foot of sidewalk, tiny sections of kerbs and gutters. Buying up this ludicrous empire was again part of Matta-Clark's project of the structural activation of severed surfaces. It is also an example of the idiosyncratic manipulation of rule-based behaviour to achieve different ends.

Along with the general reinvention of the manifold materiality of art that provided a context in which this work can be sensed, the period it was produced in was also the peak of minimal art. Whilst Matta-Clark's work is in part concerned with formalism, the application of procedures, and the revelation of structural properties, it

is precisely because his work is formally non-reductive and pur-
posely heterogenic that it is profoundly at variance with an art that
was only supposed to speak of itself and of the immaculate con-
noisseurship of its audience. This is an artwork that is exactly the
reverse of autonomous. It is openly dependent on a network of
coincidences and interconnectedness: on being seen by chance
passersby; on the receipt or avoidance of bureaucratic permissions;
on the functioning of recording devices; on good weather; on not
being discovered when acting in secret; on the theatre of its enac-
tion being an oxygenation of the still-smouldering embers of history. At the same time as it articulates a space in sculptural terms
it also complexifies it in terms of its placehood, as an object, and
within its social, chronological, and economic contexts.

Knowing that there is freedom in surprise, it is along this fault
line of rationality and the non-rational that Matta-Clark runs his
fingers—fingers which he also uses to tease another split, that
between art and architecture. Comparable to his relationship to
minimal art, rather than partaking in the functionalist urban sublime of the glass-and-steel skyscraper typified in the architecture of
Mies van der Rohe—with its interior opened to make it more gov-
ernable—Matta-Clark's work operates a dis-enclosure of urban
space: its malfunctions, voids, shadows.

The tension inherent in such spaces is portrayed well by Gilles
Deleuze in describing "any-space-whatever": the half-urban, half-
wastelands often used as sets and exteriors in post–World War II
films:

> Any-space-whatever . . . is a perfectly singular space,
> which has merely lost its homogeneity, that is, the princi-
> ple of its metric relations or the connection of its own
> parts, so that linkages can be made in an infinite number
> of ways.[2]

This tension between particularity and obliteration found in
the European bombsite translated well into the conditions in which
Matta-Clark worked out of necessity and choice: buildings eviscer-
ated by the progress of urban restructuring.

"There is a kind of complexity that comes from taking an otherwise completely normal and conventional, albeit anonymous, situation and redefining it, retranslating it into overlapping and multiple readings of conditions past and present."[3]

As an aside, this too-easy lockdown into textuality implied by the use of the word *reading* is of his time (and one replicated in perpetuity by artists hungry for the valorising seal of textual authority) but it rather understates the multiple sensory effect of the work. It is this aspect, of working with material that is in the process of being made anonymous, generic—yet turning it into an engine of connotation—that is particularly suggestive for a context that, in its apparent dematerialization, seems most likely to resist it: software.

Software lacks the easy evidence of time, of human habitation, of the connotations of familial, industrial, or office life embedded in the structure of a building. As a geometry realised in synthetic space, it is an any-space-whatever, but dry-cleaned and prised out of time.

Use of the computer happens at many levels, both hard and soft. A crucial difference with how we traditionally understand architecture, as opposed to what it is becoming under the impact of information technologies, is that everything necessarily happens at human scale—that the size, and to a certain extent the organisation, of people has a determining effect on the shape of the building. Conversely, the axiomatics that channel and produce the behaviour necessary for use of computers happen at both human and subscopic scale. The hard organs of the computer—mouse, keyboard, modem, microphone, monitor—though all matched to greater or lesser extents to human form, all snake back to the CPU.

Whilst what is of interest here is an investigation of the moment of composition between user and computer, and not a reiteration of textbook schematics, it is worth noting that simply because they occur at the level of electrons the axes of software are impossible to find for the average user. Just as when watching a film we miss out the black lines in between the frames flashing past at twenty-four per second, the invisible walls of software are designed to remain inscrutable. However, the fact that these sub-

scopic transformations of data inside the computer are simultaneously real and symbolic, where even the most abstract of theoretical terms to be found in mathematics becomes a thing, allows the
possibility of a kinaesthetic investigation—an investigation that
opens up a chance for dialogue between the smooth running of the
machine and material that might be thought of as contamination
within the terms of its devices.

Much of the "legitimate" writing and artistic production on
information technology is concerned with expanding the application of the theoretical devices used to recognise replication and
simulation (what constitutes "the real") and of those used to recognise surveillance. These themes, carried over most commonly from
debates around photography and architecture, are of course suggestive and in some cases useful, but in the easiness of their trans-
lation we should not forget that they are moving into a context that
subsumes them and is not marked by their boundaries. In acknowledging the distinct interconnectedness of the symbolic and material, this is also an approach which is opposed to the conception of
"virtuality" being taken as the desired end-state of digital technology: taking virtuality as a condition which is contained and made
possible by the actuality of digital media.

To provide the skewed access to the machines that such an
investigation requires we can siphon some fuel from the goings-on
of Gordon Matta-Clark: use faults; disturb conventions; exploit
idiosyncrasies.

Faults arise in systems when the full consequences of technical changes are not worked through before those changes are
made, or when they are deliberately covered up. This is an enormous game of hide and seek being played by a cast of millions, and
one which has wide ramifications. Perhaps the most crucial fault-
lines being traced at the moment are those around security: the
world of minutiae that compose the integrity of existence in dataspace and the way it maps back onto everyday life.[4]

The most profound restructuring of existence is taking place at
the levels of the electron and the gene. Technical complexity, commercial pressure, and the mechanisms of expression management

are blocking almost all real public discourse on the former. They are less able to do so to the latter.

Whether radical or reactionary, traditional political structures have, either deliberately or through drastic relevance-decay, abdicated almost all decision-making in these areas to commercial interests. From a similar catalogue of stock characters to that of the artist, the pariah/hero figure of the hacker has often set the pace for any critical understanding of the changes happening in and between information technologies.

Picking up a random copy of the hacker zine *2600* (Summer 1996) the scale and ramifications of issues being dealt with in this area become apparent. The contents include: an editorial on the position of hackers in the legal system and media; the code for a Linux program to block internet sites by flooding them with connection requests; a list of free phone-carriers in Australia; instructions for acquiring phone services under imaginary names; descriptions of passenger in-flight communications systems and the telecommunications infrastructures in Prague and Sarajevo; information on encryption and consumer data-security; articles on catching passwords to specific multi-user computer systems, phreaking smart pay-phones, and starting a hacker scene; the transcript of part of a court case involving the show trial of hacker Bernie S.; plus pages of small ads and letters. (Perhaps noticeable in comparing the importance of these scenes with that of art is that the second-order commentary on the work comes mainly from the media/legal system rather than just critics.)

The faults identified by hackers and others, where ethico-aesthetic situations are compounded under sheer pressure into technical ones, are implicated in wider mechanisms. These technical situations can be investigated from any point or development within these wider mechanisms, regardless of the degree of technical proficiency. Cracking open technical situations with the wider social conditions within which they occur is an increasingly necessary task. Doing so in a manner that creates a transversal relationship between different, perhaps walled-off, components, and that intimately works the technical with other kinds of material or symbolic devices is something that remains to be developed.

Tracking the faults, the severed surfaces, of technology is one way
in which this can begin to be done.

This intimacy, in addition to concerning itself with the cracks
and disjunctures, the faults in systems, can also become involved
in situations where they appear to be smoothest. For the average
user, the conventions of personal computers appear secure,
rational, almost natural, if a little awkward and tricky at times.
Like many social protocols, computer-use is a skill which users
often can't remember acquiring. Perhaps a user can remember
back to when they first got hold of a machine, when they were
waving a mouse in the air to get the cursor to move towards them;
afraid to touch the wrong key in case it damaged something; saving files all over the place; trying to draw curves in PageMaker;
inserting floppies upside-down; trying to work a cracked copy of
CuBase; learning how to conform to the machine in order to make
the machine conform to them . . .

In computer-interface design the form–function fusion is made
on the basis of averages, a focus-grouped reality based on people's
understanding of a context in which it is impossible for them to
function unless they develop the understanding already mapped
out for them. Perhaps in this context the user will always be the
ideal user, because if they are not ideal—if, within this context at
least, they do not conform to the ideal—they won't be a user at all.

Interface design is a discipline that aspires to saying nothing.
Instead of trying to crack this invisibility, one technique for investigation is to tease it into overproduction. Why use one mouse-click
when ten-thousand will do? Why use any visual information when
navigation is perfectly possible with sound alone? Why just look at
the interface—why not print it out and wear it? Why read text on
screen when a far better technology is paper? Why use a cursor
when the object you're actually pointing at can function perfectly
well to indicate the mouse position?[5]

In any other social context, what appear as protocols because
of the arbitrary nature of the machine would be revealed as man-
nerisms. (Take a fast taxi through the ruined neighbourhoods of
cyberspace by travelling through emulators of old computers:
Punch a hole in the surface of your shiny new machine by loading

up the black hole of a 1K ZX81.) When the construction of machines from the fundamental objects of the hardware—bits, bytes, words, addresses, upwards—are realised to be synthetic rather than given, or even necessarily rational (though produced through the application of rationalisation, logic) they become subject to wider possibilities for change. Software as an aggregate of very small sensory experiences and devices becomes an engine, not just of connotation, but of transformation.

Some of those transformations in occurrence can be sensed in the sheer idiosyncrasy of much software. In *The Atrocity Exhibition* and other books, J. G. Ballard mixes flat, technical descriptions of body positions as they come into composition with the synthetic geometry of architecture, automobiles, and furnishings to produce an investigation of machined erotics. He continues and intensifies the Surrealist stratagem of cutting together transgressed functionalities in order to regain entry into the order of the symbolic. To a strictly objective observer, the transitory point at which a thigh comes into convergence with a table enters into direct correlation with the way in which the original Microsoft Windows interface was bolted on top of the old DOS operating system. The tectonic impact of two neural landscapes performs an operation called progress. The software is tricked into doing something more than it was intended for. Instead of dramatic breaks, hacks and incrementally adaptive mutations are often the way things are made to move forward. (For instance, on Apple computers the desktop is already being bypassed by the absorption of some of the functions of the finder into various applications. From being a grossly over-metaphoric grand entrance hall, it has become a back alley.) When such accretions work well they are elegant, usable collages. Often they are botch jobs. In both cases, the points at which the systems mesh, collide, or repel can, at the points of confused demarcation, produce secret gardens, car parks, lamps that fuck.

Idiosyncrasies can also develop when a software system is applied to a situation in toto—perhaps most obviously, databases. The production of software dedicated to knowledge organisation and information retrieval, a field largely seen as the domain of linguists and computer scientists, immediately brings with it a range of problematics that are at once both cultural and technical. The technology underlying search engines and databases—set theory— is based on creating classifications of information according to arbitrarily or contingently meaningful schemes. It is in the application and development of those schemes with all their inevitable biases and quirks that the aesthetics of classification lies.

Attuned to quantifying, organising, isolating, drawing into relationships particular cases of the possible, and working them till they bleed some kind of relevance, databases exist firmly on the cusp of the rational and non-rational. When the Subjective Exercise Experiences Scale locks onto the Human Genome Initiative processing library stock-holding data, prepare for something approaching poetry.

Perhaps in some ways sensing into the future this destratification of conventions is the architecture of the internet. This (almost despite its position within and between various political, commercial, and bureaucratic formations) is, after all, a network which functions on a basis of being broken, continuously finding the shortest route between nodes: even as a squatter will always see the empty buildings on any street before those that are full. At these shifting, transitory points, where sensoriums intermesh, repel, clash, and resynthesize, are the possibilities for a ludic transdimensionality. Knock through a wall, and beyond the clouds of brick dust clogging up and exciting your eyes, tongue, palate, and throat, there's another universe: an empty, unclassifiable complex seething with life.

NOTES

1. Greg Bear, "Tangents," in Jack Dann & Gardner Dozois, eds., *Hackers* (New York, Ace Books, 1996), p. 222–239.

2. Gilles Deleuze, *Cinema: The Movement Image,* trans. Hugh Tomlinson and Barbara Habberjam (Minneapolis: University of Minnesota Press, 1986), p. 109.

3. Gordon Matta-Clark, quoted in Donald Wall, "Gordon Matta-Clark's Building Dissections," *Arts* magazine 50, no. 9 (May 1976), p. 76; cited in Dan Graham and Gordon Matta-Clark, *White Cube/Black Box,* ed. Sabine Breitweiser (Vienna: E. A. Generali Foundation, 1996), p. 233.

4. See Critical Art Ensemble, "The Recombinant Theatre and the Performative Matrix," in *The Electronic Disturbance* (Brooklyn, N.Y.: Autonomedia, 1994), p. 57, for a sharp political reading of how "faults" in data-collection within rigid terminological grids can be manipulated for both authoritarian and disruptive ends.

5. See various issues of I/O/D, downloadable at http://bak.spc.org/iod

A useful survey of Gordon Matta Clark's work is Pamela M. Lee, *Object to Be Destroyed* (Cambridge, MA: MIT Press, 2000)

A MEANS OF MUTATION
NOTES ON I/O/D 4: THE WEB STALKER

During 1997 and 1998 a series of legal and media confrontations were made in the United States and elsewhere. Amongst those involved were Microsoft, Netscape, and the U.S. Department of Justice. The key point of contention was whether Microsoft, a company which has a near-complete monopoly on the sale of operating systems for personal computers, had—by bundling its own web browser, Internet Explorer, with every copy of its Windows 95/98 OS—effectively blocked Netscape, an ostensible competitor in browser software,[1] from competing in a "free" market. This confrontation ran concurrently with one between Microsoft and Sun Microsystems, developers of the language Java.[2]

The "Browser Wars" involved more than these three relatively tightly constructed and similar actors, however; millions of internet users were drawn into this conflict. The nature of the proprietary-software economy meant that for any side, winning the Browser Wars would be a chance to construct the ways in which the most popular section of the internet—the world wide web—would be used, and to reap the rewards. The conflict took place in an American court and was marked by the deadeningly tedious super-formalised rituals that mark the abstraction of important decisions away from those in whose name they are made. Though the staging of the conflict was located within the legal and juridical framework of the U.S., it had ramifications wherever software is used.

Like all legalised conflicts, this was constructed in the form of a pyramidal focusing of decision. The pyramid reaches its apex with the utterance of one breath: guilty or not guilty. This almost imperceptible mote of dust at the uttermost point of the pyramid is not so important as the fact that the pyramid continues and that power is subsumed within it. The specific nature of the fleck of dust that drops from the lips of the judge has actual importance only insofar as it has the capacity to destabilise the structure.

The moment of dust is performed by processes of deletion and accretion. Those that have accreted are readily apparent; they have been documented and to some extent analysed. This is in part because it is their function to be visible—to focus the attention. The pyramid is, of course, constructed from mixed materials; some are almost incapable of combining, but they cohere to the extent that for that precious moment, and for all its reiterations, everything else is stilled.

What is deleted is every other element or dynamic that exists within the phase space of permutation surrounding that moment and that does not hurry to crush itself under the weight of that capstone.

At the same time, other shapes are being made. Other processes are occurring. Among these is the truly bastard assemblage that is the internet. At this point, the pyramid may just look something like a mountain in a cloud. The internet has been called a rhizome, but if it is one, it is one that is also wracked by organs: by backbones, by hosts, by shells, by thin filaments of cable under the waves; by its mirroring into recording devices that go under such names as Echelon.[3] But it is a shape/process under construction. It is what it is becoming, the many ways it develops in the phase space of all its possible becomings, that forms a refrain for this story.

On connecting to a URL, the user's computer sees HTML as a stream of data. This data can be formatted for use in any of a wide variety of configurations. As a current, given mediation by some interpretative device, it could even be used as a flowing pattern to determine the behaviour of a device completely unrelated to its purpose: Work it with tags? Every <HREF> could switch something on, every <P> could switch something off—administration of greater or lesser electric shocks, for instance. Most commonly, however, it is fed straight into a browser.

What are the conditions that produce this particular sort of reception facility? Three fields that are key amongst those currently conjoining to form what is actualised as the browser: economics, design, and the material. By "material" is meant the propensities of the various languages, protocols, and datatypes of the web.

If we ask, "What produces and reinforces browsing?" there is no surprise in finding the same word being used to describe recreational shopping, ruminant digestion, and the use of the world wide web. The Browser Wars form one level of consistency in the assembly of various forms of economy on the web.

Web sites are increasingly written for specific browser software, with some elements of them unreadable by other packages.[4] You get Netscape sites, Explorer sites, and sites that avoid making that split and stay at a level that both can use—and therefore consign the "innovations" of these programs to irrelevance. This situation may be considerably compounded with the introduction of customisable—and hence unusable by web-use software not correctly configured—Extensible Mark-Up Language (XML) tags.

What determines the development of this software? Demand? There is no means for it to be mobilised. Rather more likely, an arms race between on the one hand the software companies and on the other the development of passivity, gullibility, and curiosity as a culture of use of software.

One form of operation on the net that does have a very tight influence—an ability to make a classical "demand"—on the development of proprietary software for the web is the growth of online shopping and commercial information delivery. For companies on the web this is not just a question of the production and presentation of "content," but a very concrete part of their material infrastructure. For commerce on the web to operate effectively, the spatium of potential operations on the web—that is, everything that is described or made potential by the software and the network—needs to be increasingly configured towards this end.

That there are potentially novel forms of economic entity to be invented on the web is indisputable. As ever, crime is providing one of the most exploratory developers. How far these potential economic forms, guided by notions of privacy, pay-per-use, trans- and supra-nationality, etc., will develop in an economic context in which there are other actors than technical possibility, such as the state, monopolies, and so on is open to question. However, one effect of net-commerce is indisputable: Despite the role of web designers in translating the imperative to buy into a post-rave cultural experience, transactions demand contracts, and contracts demand fixed, determinable relationships. The efforts of companies on the web are focused on tying down meaning into message delivery.[5] Whilst some form of communication may occur within this mucal shroud of use-value-put-to-good-use, the focal point of the communication will always stay intact. Just click here.

Immaterial labour produces "first and foremost a social relation . . . [that] produces not only commodities, but also the capital relation."[6] If this mercantile relationship is also imperative on the immaterial labour being a social and communicative one, the position of web designers is perhaps an archetype, not just for the misjudged and cannibalistic drive for a "creative economy" currently under way in Britain, but also within a situation where a (formal) language—HTML—explicitly rather than implicitly becomes a means of production. (At one point it was vaingloriously touted as "How To Make Loot.")

Web design, considered in its wide definition—by hobbyists, artists, general-purpose temps, and specialists, and also in terms of the creation of web sites using software such as PageMill or Dreamweaver—is precisely a social and communicative practice "whose 'raw material' is subjectivity."[7] This subjectivity is an ensemble of pre-formatted, automated, contingent, and "live" actions, schemas, and decisions performed by software, languages, and designers. This subjectivity is also productive of further sequences of seeing, knowing, and doing.

A key device in the production of web sites is the page metaphor. This, of course, has its historical roots in the imaginal descriptions of the Memex and Xanadu systems, but it has its specific history in that Esperanto for computer-based documents, Structured Generalised Markup Language, and in the need for storage, distribution, and retrieval of scientific papers at CERN. Use of metaphor within computer-interface design is intended to enable easy operation of a new system by overlaying it or even confining it within the characteristics of a homely-futuristic device found outside of the computer. The metaphor can take several forms. They include emulators where, say, the entire workings of a specific synthesiser are mapped over into a computer where it can be used in its "virtual" form. The computer captures the set of operations of the synthesiser and now the term "emulation" becomes metaphorical. Allowing other modalities of use and imaginal refrain to operate through the machine, the computer now is that synthesiser—whilst also doubled into always being more. Metaphors also include items such as the familiar "desktop" "wastebasket." This is a notorious case of a completely misapplied metaphor. A wastebasket is simply an instruction for the deletion of data. Data does not, for instance, just sit and rot as things do in an actual wastebasket. That's your backup disk. Actual operations of the computer are radically obscured by this vision of it as some cosy information appliance always seen through the rear-view mirror of some imagined universal.[8]

The page metaphor in web design might as well be that of a wastebasket.

Whilst things have gone beyond maintaining and re-articulating the mode of address of arcane journals on particle physics, the techniques of page layout were ported over directly from graphic design for paper. This meant that HTML had to be contained as a conduit for channelling direct physical representation—integrity to fonts, spacing, inflections, and so on. The actuality of the networks were thus subordinated to the disciplines of graphic design and of graphical user interface simply because of their ability to deal with flatness, the screen (though there are conflicts between them based around their respective idealisations of functionality). Currently this is a situation that is already edging towards collapse as other data types make incursions onto, through, and beyond the page— but it is a situation that needs to be totalled, and done so consciously and speculatively.

Another metaphor is that of geographical references. Where do you want to go today? This echo of location is presumably designed to suggest to the user that they are not in fact sitting in front of a computer calling up files, but hurtling round an earth embedded into a gigantic trademark *N* or *e* with the power of some voracious cosmological force. The world wide web is a global medium in approximately the same way that the World Series is a global event. With book design papering over the monitor, the real processes of networks can be left to the experts in computer science . . .

It is the technical opportunity of finding other ways of developing and using this stream of data that provides a starting point for I/O/D 4: The Web Stalker. I/O/D is a three-person collective based in London.[9] As an acronym, the name stands for everything it is possible for it to stand for. There are a number of threads that continue through the group's output: a concern in practice with an expanded definition of the techniques/aesthetics of computer interface; speculative approaches to hooking these up to other formations that can be characterised as political, literary, musical, etc.; the production of stand-alone publications/applications that can fit on one high-density disk and are distributed without charge over various networks.

The material context of the world wide web for this group is viewed mainly as an opportunity rather than as a history. As all HTML is received by the computer as a stream of data, there is nothing to force adherence to the design instructions written into it. These instructions are only followed by a device obedient to them.

Once you become unfaithful to page-description, HTML is taken as a semantic markup rather than physical markup language. Its appearance on your screen is as dependent upon the interpreting device you use to receive it as on its "original" state. The actual "commands" in HTML become loci for the negotiation of other potential behaviours or processes.

Several possibilities become apparent. This data stream becomes a phase space, a realm of possibility outside the browser. It combines with another: There are thousands of other software devices for using the world wide web, waiting in the phase space of code. Since the languages are pre-existing, everything that can possibly be said in them, every program that could possibly be constructed in them, is already inherently pre-existent within them. Programming is a question of teasing out the permutations within the dimensions of specific languages or their combinations. That it is never only this opens up programming to its true power—that of synthesis.

In natural language, the fact that this text is not just a contemplation of the various potential combinations of the twenty-six letters of the alphabet is indicative of two things:

~ The immediate problem of contracting the wild fecundating dynamism of natural languages into a form in which it becomes interpretable to code (contracting in both senses, the legalistic one of construction of fixed determinate relationships, and that of making something smaller).

~ Both artificial and natural languages share a characteristic: abundance—their respective and convergent phase spaces. It is what is done with this abundance and potential for it—in literature, everyday speech, command strings—that makes things what they are and what they might become. It is the challenge and seduction of abundance that draws many people into what has been broadly framed as technoculture.

Within this phase space, perhaps one thing we are proposing is that one of the most pressing political, technical, and aesthetic urgencies of the moment is something that subsumes both the modern struggle for the control of production (that is, of energies), and the putative postmodern struggle for the means of promotion (that is, of circulation) within the dynamics of something that also goes beyond them and that encompasses the political continuum developing between the gene and the electron that most radically marks our age: the struggle for the means of mutation.

A file is dropped onto the unstuffer. The projector is opened. The hard drive grinds. The screen goes black. The blacked-out screen is a reverse nihilist moment. Suddenly everything is there.

A brief description of the functions of the Web Stalker is necessary as a form of punctuation in this context, but it can of course only be fully sensed by actual use.[10] Starting from an empty plane of colour (black is just the default mode—others are chosen using a popup menu), the user begins by marqueeing a rectangle. Using a contextual menu, a function is applied to the box. The box, a generic object, is specialised into one of the following functions. For each function put into play, one or more boxes are created and specialised.

Crawler: The Crawler is the part of the Web Stalker that actually links to the world wide web. It is used to start up, and to show the current status of the session. It appears as a window containing a bar split into three. A dot moving across the bar shows what stage the Crawler is at. The first section of the bar shows the progress of the net connection. Once connection is made and a URL is found, the dot jumps to the next section of the bar. The second section displays the progress of the Web Stalker as it reads through the found HTML document looking for links to other URLs. The third section of the bar monitors the Web Stalker as it logs all the links that it has found so far. Thus, instead of the user being informed that connection to the net is vaguely "there" by movement on the geographic TV-style icon in the top right-hand corner, the user has access to specific information about processes and speeds.

Map: Map displays references to individual HTML documents as circles, and the links from one to another as lines. The URL of each document can be read by clicking on the circle it is represented by. Once a web session has been started at the first URL opened by the Crawler, Map moves through all the links from that site, then through the links from those sites, and so on. The mapping is dynamic—"Map" is a verb rather than a noun.

Dismantle: The Dismantle window is used to work on specific URLs within HTML documents. URLs at this level will be specific resources such as images, email addresses, sound files, downloadable documents, etc. Clicking and dragging a circle into the Dismantle window will display all URLs referenced within the HTML document you have chosen, again in the form of circles and lines.

Stash: The Stash provides a document format that can be used to make records of web use. Saved as an HTML file it can also be read by "browsers" and circulated as a separate document. Sites or files are included by dragging and dropping URL circles into a Stash.

HTML Stream: HTML Stream shows all of the HTML as it is read by the Web Stalker in a separate window. Because as each link is followed by the crawler the HTML appears precisely as a stream, the feed from separate sites is effectively mixed.

Extract: Dragging a URL circle into an Extract window strips all the text from a URL. It can be read on screen in this way or saved as a text file.

Of course, no statement of function, whilst satisfactorily acting as a notice of concrete reality that serves to attract and displace energies and dynamics of many sorts, is ever sufficient. If they work, such constructions are always spilling over and mobilising more.

The Web Stalker performs an inextricably technical, aesthetic, and ethical operation on the HTML stream that at once refines it, produces new methods of use, ignores much of the data linked to or embedded within it, and provides a mechanism through which the deeper structure of the web can be explored and used.

This is not to say much. It is immediately obvious that the Stalker is incapable of using images and some of the more complex functions available on the web. These include, for instance, GIFs, forms, Java, VRML, and frames. Some of these are deliberately ignored as a way of breaking the dependence on the page and producing a device that is more suited to the propensities of the network. Some are left out simply because of the conditions of the production of the software—we had to decide what was most important for us to achieve with the available resources and time. This is not to say that if methods of accessing this data were to be incorporated into the Stalker they would have been done so "on their own terms." It is likely that at the very least they would have been dismantled, dissected, opened up for use in some way.

Another key factor in the shape of the program and the project as a whole is the language it was written in: Lingo, the language within Macromedia Director, a program normally used for building multimedia products and presentations. This is, to say the least, a gawky angle from which to approach writing any application. But it was used for several reasons: because it gave us very good control over interface design, and because NetLingo was just being introduced, but more important, because within the skill-base of I/O/D, that was what we had. That it was done anyway is, we hope, an encouragement to those who have the "wrong" skills and few resources but a hunger to get things done, and a provocation to those who are highly skilled and equipped but never do anything.

Whilst the Web Stalker's mode of production was independent, its modes of circulation were as heterogeneous as possible. Previous issues of I/O/D were aimed at relatively small though diffuse underground networks of distribution. They got around extremely well by word of mouth and not much more. This time, because we thought the project was timely and of potential interest to a wider range of people, we adopted a strategy of attempting to assimilate to or impose the project on a variety of discourse networks and movements. These included discourses with established media structures and institutions, but also more tentative, non-codified cultures of use that emerge around software programs.

Previous to the Web Stalker, work by artists on the web was channelled into providing content for web sites. These sites are bound by the conventions enforced by browser-type software. They therefore remain the most determining aesthetic of this work. The majority of web-based art, if it deals with its media context at all, can be understood by four brief typologies:

~ incoherence (user abuse, ironic dysfunctionality, randomness to mask pointlessness)

~ archaeology (media archaeology, emulators of old machines and software, and structuralist materialist approach)

∿ retro-tooling (integrity to old materials in "new" media, integrity as kitsch derived from punk/jazz/hip-hop, old-style computer graphics, and "filmic references"—the Futile Style of London[11])

∿ deconstruction (conservative approach to analysing-in-practice the development of multimedia and networks, consistently rearticulating contradiction rather than using it as a launching pad for new techniques of composition)

Within the discourse networks of art, including critical technique; license to irresponsibility; compositions-in-progress of taste stratification and breaks; institutions; finance; individual survival strategies; media; social networks; legitimation devices; openness to new forms; and avowed attentiveness to manifestations of beauty, there were dynamics that were useful to mobilise in order to open up possibilities of circulation and effect for the Web Stalker. However, while the project was situated within contemporary art it is also widely operative outside of it. Most obviously it is, at the very least, a piece of software. How can this multiple position be understood by an art world that is still effectively in thrall to the notion of the autonomy of the object?

Anti-art is always captured by its purposeful self-placement within a subordinate position to that which it simply opposes. Alternately, the deliberate production of non-art is always an option but not necessary in this context. (Let those crumbs fall off the table, they look starved.) Instead, this project produces a relationship to art that at times works on a basis of infiltration or alliance, and at others simply refuses to be excluded by it and thus threatens to reconfigure entirely what it is part of. The Web Stalker is art. Another possibility, therefore, emerges. Alongside the categories art, anti-art, and non-art, something else spills over: not-just-art.

Of course, once this ploy is opened and proliferates it becomes apparent that it quickly colonises all of what sees itself as art and nothing but simply by virtue of acknowledging its integration into other systems—of valorisation, decoration, sociality, etc. By the same token it also opens up what is categorised as non-art to the descriptive, critical, de-responsibilising and other potentially less fruitful qualities and operations of art. Tormented by wanna-be-loved negativism, anti-art as a category subsumed within art just about retains its desk at the Ministry of Culture.

Just as the Stalker is not-just-art, it can only come into occurrence by being not just itself. It has to be used. Assimilation into possible circuits of distribution and effect in this case means something approaching a media strategy.

"For modernist intellectuals, cultural capital or distinction in Bourdieu's sense varies inversely with one's contact with the media."[12]

Operating at another level to the Web Stalker's engagement within art were two other forms of media which were integral to the project: stickers (bearing a slogan and the I/O/D URL) and free-ware. Both are good contenders for being the lowest, most despised grade of media. That the Web Stalker is freeware has been essential in developing its engagement with various cultures of computing.

The Stalker is currently being downloaded at a rate of about a thousand copies per week. Responses have ranged from intensely detailed mathematical denunciations of the Map and total outrage that anyone should try anything different, to evil glee and a superb and generous understanding of the project's techniques and ramifications.

Whilst for many the internet simply is what is visible with a browser, at the same time it is apparent that there is a widespread desire for new non-formulaic software. One of the questions that the Stalker poses is how program design is taken forward. Within the limitations of the programming language and those of time, the project achieved what it set out to do. As a model of software development outside of the super-invested proprietary one this speculative and interventional mode of production stands along-side two other notable radical models: that of Free Software[13] and that derived from the science shops (wherein software is developed by designers and programmers in collaboration with clients for specifically social uses). Unlike these others, it is not so likely to find itself becoming a model that is widely adoptable and sustainable.

In a sense, then, the Web Stalker works as a kind of "tactical software,"[14] but it is also deeply implicated within another kind of tacticity—the developing street-knowledge of the nets. This is a sense of the flows, consistencies, and dynamics of the nets that is most closely associated with hackers, but that is perhaps immanent in different ways in every user.

Bringing out and developing this culture, however, demands attention. In some respects this induction of idiosyncratic knowledges of minute effects ensures only that whilst the Browser Wars will never be won, they are never over. So long as there's the software out there working its temporal distortion effects on "progress" . . . so long as there's always some nutter out there in the jungle tooled up with some VT-100 web viewer, copies of Mosaic, MacWeb, whatever . . .

At the same time we need to nurture our sources of this *ars metropolitani* of the nets. During recent times, and most strongly because of the wider effects of specific acts of repression, hacking itself has often become less able to get things going because it has (a) been driven more underground, (b) been offered more jobs, and (c) been less imaginatively willing or able to ally itself with other social currents.

Software forges modalities of experience—sensoriums through which the world is made and known. As a product of "immaterial labour," software is a social, technical, and aesthetic relation that is embodied—and that is at once productive of more relations. That the production of value has moved so firmly into the terrain of immaterial labour, machine-embodied intelligence, style as factory, the production of subjectivity, makes the evolution of what was previously sectioned as "culture" so much more valuable to play for—potentially always as sabotage—but, as a development of the means of mutation, most compellingly as synthesis.

Synthesis is explicitly not constitutive of a universe of synchronisation and equivalence where everything connects to everything. It promises nothing but reconstitutive obliteration to "worlds" where everything means only one thing: virtual office, virtual pub, virtual gallery, virtual nightclub—however many more sonic gulags passing as virtual mixing-decks. What is so repulsive about this nailed-down faithfulness is not so much that its dark side is about as disturbing as a black-light bulb, or that it presents a social terrain which has been bounced clean by the most voracious of doormen— the miserable consciousnesses of its producers—but that it is continually dragging this space of composition, network, computer, user, software, socius, program production, back into the realm of representation, the dogged circular churning of avatars through the palace of mundane signs, stiffs reduced if at all possible to univocal sprites, rather than putting things into play, rather than making something happen.

Synthesis incorporates representation as a modality. Representation is not replaced but subsumed by the actualisation of ideas and the dynamism of material through which, literally "in the realm of possibility," it becomes contingent. But this is not to trap synthesis within the "inherent" qualities of materials. "Truth to materials" functions at once as both a form of transcendence through which by the purest of imputations interpretative schema can pluck out essences and as a form of repressively arch earnestness. This is a process of overflowing all ideal categories.

The Map makes the links between HTML documents. Each URL is a circle, every link is a line. Sites with more lines feeding into them have brighter circles—filched data corruscating with the simple fact of how many and which sites connect to boredom.com, extreme.net, or wherever. (Unless it's been listed on the ignore.txt file, customisable and tucked into the back of the Stalker.) Every articulation of the figure composing itself on screen is simply a link being followed through. The map spreads out flat in every direction, forging connections rather than faking locations. It is a figuration that is immutably live—a processual opening-up of the web that, whilst it deals at every link with a determinate arrangement, has no cutoff point other than infinity. Whilst the browser just gives you history under the Go menu, the Map swerves past whichever bit of paper is being pressed up to the inside of the screen to govern the next hours of click-through time by developing into the future—picking locks as it goes.

From there, in unison with whichever of the other functions are applied, a predatory approach to data is developed. Sites are dismantled, stored, scanned to build up other cultures of use of the nets. That the software is cranky, that things become alien, that it is not the result of years of flowcharted teams, that it forces PC users to use Alt-Ctrl-Delete (horrific act!) to quit the program is not in question.

All the while, synthesis keeps running, keeps mixing—producing sensoriums, modes of operation, worldviews that are downloadable (that is, both traceable and open), mixable, measurable, assimilable (but not without risk of contamination), discardable, perhaps even immersive. This is a poetics of potential that is stringent—not just providing another vector for perpetually reactive opportunism—yet revelling in the possibility always also operating within the most intensified sounds: a hardcore methodology.

Aggregates are formed from the realm induced by the coherence of every possibility. Syntactics tweaks, examines, and customs them according to context. This context is not pre-formatted. It is up for grabs, for remaking. Synthesis determines a context within which it is constitutive and comes into composition within ranges of forces. Everything—every bit, every on or off fact—is understood in terms of its radical coefficiency, against the range of mutation from which it emerged and amongst the potential syntheses with which it remains fecund. It is the production of sensoria that are productive not just of "worlds" but of the world.

NOTES

1. Only an *ostensible* competitor because the browsers produced by Netscape and Microsoft are so nearly identical that they form not an economic but a technical and aesthetic monopoly. The

release of the source code for Netscape Navigator under the name Mozilla has not significantly changed this situation.

2. Again, because of its near-monopoly over PC operating systems, Microsoft was able to set the terms—against previously made agreements—on which Java would be developed. It is widely agreed that Microsoft—and to some extent, Sun—significantly compromised the actual and potential power of the language.

3. Resources on the Echelon system are available at http://www.xs4all.nl/~konfront   and   http://caq.com/CAQ/ CAQBackIssues.htm

4. For instance, the I/O/D shout tag. <IOD4> is a HTMLish element that is only recognised by the Web Stalker. Usage: <IOD4 [attributes]> (there is no closing tag for this element). Attributes: The Web Stalker will read your HTML document and display your "SHOUT" message in a field in the top left of the Web Stalker window. (<IOD4 SHOUT="any text you want displayed to Web Stalker users">.) This message can't be read by web "browsers," so make the most of it.

5. See, for instance, the skirmishes around name ownership produced in the net.art hijacking of corporate names by Heath Bunting   and   Rachel   Baker   at   irational.org (http://www.irational.org), or at the other extreme the attempts at the technical introduction of a precise indexicality when a brand name is typed into a browser by Centraal (http://www.real-names.com).

6. Maurizio Lazzarato, "Immaterial Labor," in Michael Hardt and Paul Virno, *Radical Thought in Italy: A Potential Politics* (Minneapolis: Minnesota University Press, 1996), p. 142.

7. Ibid., p. 142.

8. The device's advantage is in its ease of use—compared, for instance, to the tiresome DELETE command in DOS—rather than any "natural" affiliation with this metaphor.

9. Simon Pope, Colin Green, Matthew Fuller.

10. The I/O/D home page, from which all the group's output is available (including PC and Macintosh versions of the Web Stalker), is provided by Backspace: http://www.backspace.org/iod

11. See FSOL section on I/O/D site.

12. Mark Poster, *The Second Media Age* (Cambridge, U.K.: Polity Press, 1997), p. 5.

13. Free Software Foundation: http://www.fsf.com

The reasons the I/O/D did not in this case follow the FSF model of free software are relatively simple. Whilst as a structure it undoubtedly works and we are supportive of it, it is an economy that demands a developing critical mass to work. This is happening for programmers working with larger computers. With the increasing use of Linux (see Linus Torvald's home page: http://www.earthspace.net/ ~ esr/faqs/linus), it is also happening for personal computers, which is the scale we are working on. However, there is no comparable economy working for the exchange of Lingo code. This is, of course, because Director is designed to produce hermetically sealed routines called "projectors." If the code for the Stalker was to have been distributed under Copyleft, there would have been no way of enforcing that its use continue to remain open, as this is such an easy method of invisible incorporation.

14. See "The ABC of Tactical Media," Geert Lovink and David Garcia: http://www.waag.org/tmn/

See also Michel de Certeau, *Culture in the Plural* (Minneapolis: Minnesota University Press, 1997), p. viii.

BREAK THE LAW OF INFORMATION
NOTES ON SEARCH ENGINES
AND NATURAL SELECTION[1]

BACK UP

There is no permanent backup device for the internet. A number
of institutions have made one-off synchronous copies of the web
that claim to be complete for the duration of the period it takes
their spiders to reach the furthest corners of the web.[2] There are
also systems which actively monitor every email or newsgroup
message sent on behalf of the odder fans of political action and dis-
solution.[3] But of course both of these are partial. As what Gregory
Ulmer has usefully called "a pre-broken system," the net has no
centralised backup. Copies of *elements* of the net are backed up
across thousands of storage devices off and across itself. Were the
whole lot to go down, putting back together the results of such dis-
graceful degradation would be an insane task.

Inevitably, some large areas of the web would slide back into
place with the efficiency of a file amongst filing cabinets. Others
however—made on the fly, left without a double—would go missing. Still more would have their links tangled, lost—a mess of
stringy, gloopy, gone data.

Natural Selection[4] is in a sense the result of this crash before it happens. It is the web picked up in pieces by people who never made
it, put back together in a way that makes more sense. It is obvious

69

that the British Airports Authority site would "want" to link to information about people getting killed by anti-immigration police.[5] It is obvious that someone looking for information on fertility treatments would want to find a site mixing the histories of different acts of racial "improvement" into a corporate brochure. And it is obvious that anyone looking for traces of overtly racialised political activism on the net is going to want their browser to become infested by a fast-breeding Jamaican virus in the guise of a triple-consciousnessed poet.[6]

BLACK BOX

A search engine is a black box. That is to say, the relationship between its input and output is masked. The tension between making a search engine usable, predictable, and "refinable," and the commercial necessity of maintaining its constituent algorithms and processes as proprietary information, provides one of the key contexts for this project.

Piracy of any electronic technology is usually carried out by reverse-engineering: feeding it inputs and monitoring its output until a tabulation of its workings can be drawn up. The black box is not actually cracked open and scrutinised, but is fed line after line until it can be simulated.

What is true of the search engine is also true of the user. When you use HotBot, for instance, your search string and all the results you click on are logged and recorded along with your domain and IP address.

This information is useful for many reasons, and it becomes increasingly so over time with repeated use. It allows the more accurate targeting of search results to specific enquiry entries (according to frequency of choice) and advertising (according to proportional interest from certain domains). Any impression that engines are there to provide a useful service financed by incidental advertising is of course pure "company history," as Yahoo puts it.

Just as the engine helpfully provides a field in which you can type in your search string, the engine is also opening up an aperture through which the user can be interrogated. There are always at least two black boxes in this equation. The interface is where they meet and engineer each other.

Natural Selection sits on top of any one of the mainstream search engines, filtering their results and, if certain strings are fed to it, slipping in a result from the bottom of the deck. The work is composed by making an interface to an interface. The user comes to the engine and presents a search string, a history of others and an internet location. The composition is driven by the lure of access to data. As they come together, the various elements, devices, and drives produce a double-blinded bait-and-switch.

It is this context—of the specific rules of formation, of the grammars of information put into play by various search engines— that Natural Selection operates in, and in which this story hopes to open up a little.

INFORMATION TRANSFERENCE

Shannon:[7] The amount of information in a message is in proportion to its unpredictability.

Of course, this definition of information defines it in strict relation to the context in which it is received. It is strictly relativist. (It provides one of the crucial problems for designers of search engines attempting to produce a machine-enforced dialogism, where the information derived by each user is the result of an ongoing process of discrimination that can be stored in a database. The various ways in which a user can create a "my" version of various engines-become-portals are examples of one approach to this problem.)

This definition of information has important implications for the construction of search engines. The search engine is absolutely unable to treat a word or any collection of symbols entered into it in a contextualised manner; there are ways of refining or narrowing down the search, of course, but the core of what it has to act upon is the string of characters that it has just been requested to find matches or correspondences for.

One response to this has been to produce a situation where the user has the responsibility to do the thinking for the engine. Yahoo, for instance, prides itself on its "ontology"—its super-mainstream view of the world. Users too, as members of a conformist society, are expected to have internalised this ontology, but also to be able to use it reflexively. That is to say, the learned and assumed conformism of the user can be operated upon by them, tweaked, at the same time as it is being used to get to the required link.

This is not to say that this internalised conformism has an open architecture in the case of either the user or the engine—both present to each other as black boxes—but rather that what Natural Selection does is in a sense make manifest the production of this double consciousness and open it to some form of reconfiguration.

A directory-based system, such as Yahoo, uses human operators to classify different sites according to a pre-ordained hierarchy of terms. To greater or lesser extents, systems which don't use them, relying on full automation, avoid this conformism, largely, as is examined more fully later, to the degree that they attempt to ascribe, involve, or invent semantic meaning in the fields on which they operate. To the degree at which it occurs, the refusal of making straightforward sense by the engine becomes the best tool by whose help the most secret components of the net can be opened.[8] Here, the occurrence of information in Shannon's sense, veering towards its upper limit of utter randomness, is limited solely by the congruence of search strings.

At the same time, their avoidance of overt taxonomisation of the world—their heightened level of information in this sense— means that the development of a search-consciousness, perhaps a temporary micro-subject thrown together by the agglomeration of strings, results, and guesses into a briefly memorised sensorium, remains trapped at the level of articulation of that loaded bane of software culture—intuition. A more sustained, distributed, inquisitive, or conflictual sensorium demands more difficult and supple ways to cohere.

THE COPY JUMPED

One other definition for the amount of information in a sentence, object, or process is the length of the set of instructions—the program—necessary to make a copy or model of it.[9] A game of cricket has more information than a game of knuckles. A paper cup has more information than a plain sheet of paper. By this definition, at least, the internet is very high in information. To create a set of instructions to copy it would be just short of impossible.

What Natural Selection does is, in a sense, just that: It turns the internet into a copy of itself. This denaturalised selection treats the net as something picked up on the street. Found, it doubles itself when examined: mangy paint-dripped goat; soup can; planet. The instructions for its copying are found in every line of code that makes it up.

However massified the net becomes, however much "diversity" is attached, Natural Selection always adds one more bit, one last line that, instead of adding information to the net, will always force the cognisance of its own grounding incompleteness. Thus at once, the copy will never be made—the thing has to be done for real.

CONDENSATION

The search string, the series of symbols tapped into the search field on the search engine, like the password for the hacker, draws all the protocols and machines in onto itself as an act of condensation. In common with elements within indexes, search terms are words or numbers disengaged from direct social or linguistic involvement. The string of characters constructs itself as an aperture to alignment with a potentially infinite amount of interlocutions, the key around which a thousand locks ensconce their levers. For the second or so that it is typed, all of this potential is under pressure. From the moment that the search command is given, the string and its ramifications begins to extrude. An arbitrary wad of bits heats temporarily up into a larval plasticity that has it tonguing for the contradictory, the useless, and the lost.

What Natural Selection does is to maintain this sense of plasticity. When the search string is entered, it is under a pressure that is not let up as the results pile up by percentages onto the page. Rather than each result providing a smooth transition from risk, from information, into assuredness, it becomes evident that every link is articulated in many ways. The switch-tongue is in constant spasm. It is in this state that a politics of the switches and of the string can be made.

FORMS

One of the mundane ways in which the web has been found to be most "useful" is in the ability to construct forms which can be filled out online. This, a capacity from early versions of HTML onwards, is again the creation of a reading aperture into the user. Feeding into databases, they "traverse and cancel" the already questionable "public/private distinction"[10] by a literal interrelation. A question implies an incomplete picture of reality which an answer completes. In this case, however, ticking checkboxes implies an addition to reality—an accumulatory combination of positives which individually and together combine to produce form in numbers.

In *The Temple of Confessions* and their related techno-ethnographic internet work,[11] Guillermo Gómez-Peña and Roberto Suifentes use this shape-making facility of forms to entice the self-production of fear and desire about Chicanos and Mexicans in U.S. art and net audiences. The confessions of fear and desire pour into a database where they form a switch tongue-writhing in a perpetual glottal roar of confusion, hate, and fantastical need.

In comparison, Natural Selection takes this database of fear and desire as already pre-existing—as the entire net. One of the modes in which elements of Natural Selection operates is a reverse of what Gómez-Peña calls the "Dantean model of multiculturalism,"[12] in which the flaneur from the North descends to the South to sample the strictly localised flavour. Here, Euro-American technoculture is exoticised and given the mumbo-jumbo status it hungers for but can never attain. The accumulatory combination of positives produces a weight in data, a gravitational pull that turns conceptions of what constitutes marginality inside-out.

ENTER A TOURIST, LEAVE A LOCAL

Web work is endless. Why do something as text when you can do it as sound? Why do it as mere sound when you can do it as a real-time post-raster 3D walkthrough intentional community with bad-word filtering and ambient billboards?

If the net is already a copy, then to double it demands a constitutional heterogeneity that is nothing if not a mess. The founding statements of Romanticism demanded a radical incompleteness, a cursed restlessness against the apparent foreclosures of industrialisation. Such a "refusal of closure" is the condition of work for all those who put bread on the table by shovelling content and code onto servers. But with grinding ambivalence it is also found realised in a reversioned form as the widely popularised conceptual device of the rhizomatic network. Such refusal of finitude is both an incomprehensible glimpse over the abyss for regulators and those in need of the reassurance of "critical understanding," and the excuse for extending overtime into your sleep. It is inherent in the texture and dynamics of the web, and forms the swamp on which Natural Selection is grounded.

This mess sprawls out in several ways: in terms of distribution across the net and position within different server-regimes; in terms of producing work for machine readerships; in terms of working many technico-aesthetic approaches simultaneously; and clearly, in terms of authorship.

Much has been made of the potential on the net for small groups of people or individuals to develop visibility or presence equal to major companies or institutions, often to usurp vertical-hold over their public image. This was especially the case in the early- to mid-nineties. Later, as the web-design market restructured along rationalised lines, the corporate influx onto the net became an increasingly normalised procedure, and new forms of software and increasing production times raised barriers to making ostensibly corporate sites, various groups developed ways of destabilising the apparent authorship of sites. Many of these remained strictly on the level of swapping zeros for ones and standing back to admire the—inevitably invisible—confusion and collect the letters from the lawyers. Others, however, knotted themselves more intimately and uncomfortably into the political and technical fabric of representation and communication.[13]

When dealing with such a diffuse dynamic as racialisation, pressing attention solely on a specific target is not necessary. Being able to deal with it in as many ways and as many places as it exists is. Inevitably this means relinquishing the appearance of "clarity" essential to validation in terms of art in order to turn more than one kind of purism into more matter for mongrelisation.

Doubling the web demands that glib coffee-table web design becomes an appearance along with default-grey file directories, that rainbow-coloured, <blink>-heavy home pages get bitten along with customer service-oriented, purchase-opportunity-provision-included product-information displays. At the same time as one mode of operation within Natural Selection is to produce a destabilisation of the apparent reliability of racialised sites by hooking their familiar routines into heritage free-fall, it is equally imperative that other dynamics come through.

There are around twenty sites that sit directly after the initial sub-directory in the site URL. They come from people working in different countries, different political, narrative, and interactive angles. Many kinds of personal histories are in operation alongside approaches to users and interrelationships with elements of the web that they link themselves into or cut themselves off from. The Natural Selection front end, the doctored search engine, is a specific technical and cultured intervention, a hack, into "a culture that has no culture"—information science—in order to tease out what it represses and what it produces. Making this break into the net produces a surplus of possibility—we could do anything with it—that allows others to take it on as an opportunity. This surplus produced by a technical and conceptual break—what might happen if you could begin to sense the politics of algorithms whilst you used them?—allows a multitude of aesthetics, experiences, voices, flows, positions, and lives to operate interconnectedly and in parallel without making them conform to any particular model of operation.

Different kinds of energies, different speeds, are also capable of mobilisation in a process of work that is not overdetermined by a finalised shape: energy from hate, derision, communication, stupidity; programming energy; research. For a long while this meant that some of it never climbed out of Beta, but it also means that it produces an extended period of experimentation that can never be quite over. This drawn-out, not-quite-programmatic dispersal of working over time that is inherent in all kinds of work on the web is also echoed in the distribution of the component sites across it.

Natural Selection is composed of many sites. All of them are accessible via the search engine, as they are via any other search engine. Only a proportion of them are pushed to be indexed on the ostensible front-end as "Star Sites." Forming a constellation of sites on and off the mongrel domain (with varying thicknesses of cross-linking it never appears as a whole) there is no complete index, no climbing up the URL to find the answer. Some of it may never get seen by users, but will be constantly read by crawlers and agents. In any work on the internet, machines both hard and soft are the primary audience.

BRIGHT LATTICES OF LIGHT UNFOLDING AGAINST THE COLOURLESS VOID

In one software millionaire's mansion, the walls are covered not with paintings but with flatscreen monitors linked to a voice-activated database of images. Any time a conversation occurs in some part of the house the screens change to reflect it. The millionaire coos to his baby son whilst feeding him a bottle and dictating a memo into a phone. Some cracked-up old madonna and child appears, a ball game, gouache cowboys, pulmonary cancer on ultrasound, then 3-D NASDAQ flows texture-mapped to a family snap taken on the lawn. Mummy herself enters to usher in a group of business associates and take baby away. Courbet's studio appears. The naked model is clad in a seasonally updated business suit. Something transcendental from *National Geographic*. Talk moves on; the computer reads every word uttered, flashing up a picture corresponding to any one of thousands of keywords from the database; everyone affects not to notice.

The web sites produced as part of Natural Selection involve the mobilisation of words that have become crystallised forms of racialisation. Typing a search string into the Natural Selection search engine either allows you access to the net as usual, or, should you enter one of several thousand keywords, clicking on an apparently transparent search result drops you into its double.

Imagining into the lexical space of the fear, desire, hate, and will to control and define that composes racialisation allows the registration of a shape composed in crisis by language. The accumulation of shifting populations of terms of abuse, of jargon, of political or scientific code, of euphemisms, agglomerates into conceptual and signifying phase forms. Networks of potholes and caverns under the homogenised surface of mediatised language are opened up for rearticulation and engineering.

This occurs not just as an incursion into enemy mind-space by a punitive band of artists with the oxygen-tent souls of angels, but as a response to senses of what might be done and as the public development of models that might be taken further.

.sitUATE

Two models that feed into Natural Selection are conjoined by use of the same string of characters to mark kinds of poiesis, making, that are attractive by both their livid intensity and their attempts at critical technics. For Guy Debord, writing before the formation of the Situationist International (S.I.), the construction of situations was "the concrete construction of momentary ambiences of life and their transformation into a superior passional quality."[14] Situations were to be something produced in the city, in real space. For Donna Haraway, writing about feminist scientific practice, situated knowledge is equally "rooted in yearning, not an abstract philosophical foundation."[15]

Tensions exists between the two uses of the same sign. Debord insists on a practice that provokes the release of "primary sentiments."[16] Haraway, involved in writing which still has to contend with determinist scientisms whose agenda is very much the "discovery" (and political use) of such compulsive drives, proposes instead the practices that are "suspicious, implicated, knowing, ignorant, worried, and hopeful."[17]

Writing after the foundation of the S.I. about what is intended by situations, there is what might be taken as an almost literal description of certain aspects of Natural Selection: "We are not going to limit ourselves . . . with environments of mechanistically provoked surprises."[18] Clearly, entering a search string and finding that it takes you not to the hoped-for home page of the European Skinhead Army but to some pervert nonsense looking too much like the real thing to be quite reassuringly wrong enough for comfort is exactly that. You're tricked by a few lines of code. What can clearly be seen, though, in both the preparation and execution of this project is that, " . . . setting up, on the basis of more or less clearly recognised desires, a temporary field of activity favourable to those desires"[19] is not quite so simple—this could be the description of a business plan. Situated knowledge is for Haraway something equally particular, but complicated by embodiment, by "sometimes painful" processes of building relationships, structures, and accountability into the process. What unites both forms, the "construction of situations" and "situated knowledge," however, is the urgency of and the possibility for establishing concrete freedoms via genuine experiment.

Correctly understanding the "merely empirical experimentalism"[20] of the academic avant-garde to be rigidifying and pre-determinate of outcome in the manner of heavily disciplined scientific procedure,[21] Debord criticises experimental work which seeks only to operate within pre-established conceptual categories. Haraway lives in an altogether trickier space, which (although it is at least partly in the grip of an academic feminism which has to make the most tortuous excuses before it feels permitted to crack a joke, but feels quite at liberty to punish the world with grimly didactic allegorical paintism as book covers) seeks to establish intermeshing and conflictual fields of lived experience, scientific method, political mobilisation, diffusion of knowledges in order to go beyond and change them. The making of alliances, something which is inherent to the composition of Mongrel, a group of artists founded on messing with the codes of race, technology, and intelligence, demands concrete practices of learning and accountability in order to make the connections that it desires. For, "if they are not so bound, connection and coalition disintegrate into orgies of moralism"[22]—something profoundly familiar to post-situationist shufflers. It is this thickness of connection in the work—a situatedness of lived relations instead of identity—rather than any access to primal realities, that we believe allows the combination of machines and people to make concrete both a refusal of slavery and access to life.

INSTRUCTIONS

In search engines using automatic indexing to produce inverted files—the number of occurrences of a word related to the number of occurrences of all words in the file—an apparent transparency is generated by the simple procedure of pulling the words directly from the sites that they log. What is important, what is notable, appears simply by virtue of being logged by the crawler. Inevitably, this flat perspective produces an outcry about quality control. For information science, "it is entirely possible that vast concatenations of information resources are just not susceptible to any really effective measure of control and access, at least not by any automatic procedures applied on a large scale."[23] The web challenges not only the status of the document, the corpus, but also the index. This challenge is the result of an attempt to refuse, or at least avoid, the burden of classification built into the architecture of the web.

The Uniform Resource Locator (URL) of the world wide web is an attempt to "point to any document (or any other type of resource) in the universe of information"[24] without *a priori* specification of the resource within any system of classification. Within this schema, anything that is digitizable can be stored, networked, and located. The architecture of the WWW is an attempt to route around classification, or at least provide a situation where many such interpretative formations can operate without universalisation. This is embedded not just in the device of the URL but also in details such as the simple geek idealism of the difference between physical and logical styles (where, in the latter, the site designer can specify that the individually determined settings of the user's browser can determine the way to display certain forms of text emphasis). The WWW attempts to produce a "preconceptual"[25] technology that—in a similar way to a computer's memory, storing both the data it uses and the programs the data is used with—produces a field within which concepts coexist alongside the rules to which the field is subjected.

Elsewhere there has been discussion of how particular modes of use of HTML have tended to lock down the potential of the network into an idealised form of paper-based media.[26] Here, though, I hope to move towards a consideration of how the rules of formation that operate in the construction of search engines produce many particular overt or anonymous ways of making and using the web. It is not suggested that these are secret rules for the confabulation of the world beyond the magic gate internet into something that it is not, nor are they necessarily merely illusions, misinformation, bad habits of thought, but a series of perceptual devices which are themselves reliant on and interwoven with others—and which are as such open to reinvention.

THE EATING

Within computer science there is argument as to the verification of the accuracy of both hardware and software. Donald McKenzie, whose work has focused on the sociology of "proof," suggests that there are three identifiable positions in the debate: " . . . the formal, mechanised verification of programs and hardware designs; the denial that verification confers certainty akin to that conferred by proof in mathematics; and the advocacy of human, rather than machine, proof."[27] There is a triangulation of tension here between the relative status of verification and proof and between mathematics performed by humans and by machines.

Software and hardware are relied upon not only for matters of life and death, but for financial and military operations. Inevitably, then, the need to determine the correct expression of an accurate result—and within software, concatenations of millions of results— has produced, if not agreement as to what constitutes accuracy, at least variable standards of proof. (The U.K. Ministry of Defence, for instance, distinguishes between a "formal proof" and a "rigor-

ous argument" in its specifications for the assessment of mission-
critical software.[28])

These arguments are played out at a "lower" level in the construction of search engines. However, the accuracy of results
returned is impossible to check because of the proprietary closure
of search engines' programming. They are also complicated by
their interface between social and technical protocols. For users,
getting sense out of search engines is empirically based—deductive
rather than inductive. For search engines, getting sense, or at least
data, out of the web is based around three major strategies.

Directories trade on their particular take on the web. Yahoo!,
for instance, gathers URLs largely from people submitting their
own web sites for classification, but also from Yahoo!'s own
crawler software. Each site is then classified by an employee who
places the site into one of several thousand sub-categories. What
started out as the ironically named "Yet Another Hierarchically
Ordered Ontology" but, that being too revealing, swiftly became
just another yelping logo.gif of capitalised joy, is able in this way to
bunch results together into classes. Because the system refers to
digital documents rather than books on a shelf, it also allows the
possibility of having sites stored in the crosshairs of several different classifications. However, because they sell themselves on and
operate by a claim to be able to at once abstract the essence of all
things and at the same time conform as accurately as possible to
the expectations of their statistically idealised user, the terms on
which they classify are rendered solely by a normalised idea of
"subject." Just as search engines can only operate given the pre-
standardisation of language and spelling already put into place over
several centuries by printed documents, directories assume a conceptual normativity. The "subject" or "topic" of a web site is what
it is really talking about, its essence. It is not classified by whatever
conscious or unconscious machine propels its production; by its
use of background color #A5C679; by that which it makes allegorical reference to; or by that which forms the centre of its coming
into existence but which it is unable to name. Constructing a directory is, of course, complicated by the existence of contradictory or
completely incommensurable schemas, but this becomes a negligi-

ble problem after it is understood that the clear asymmetry between such systems and the world ensures that the only moment any directory becomes completely stable is also the moment that everything dies.

One pact between terminal equilibrium and the sustained recursion of the-same-but-different is formulated as the theory of quality: of establishing a mechanism by which certain levels of scientific discipline; relevance; erotic intensity; rarity; legal, commercial, or other forms of trustworthiness; timeliness, and so on can be reliably guaranteed. Perhaps as simple would be to have search engines organised not by exactitude of match by subject, but by degree of absolutely determined irrelevance.

If directories promise nothing less than the ultimate victory of common sense over difference, the two broad types of semantic network in use to produce search engines rely on far less explicit ways of codifying the web. Before establishing what these are, it is worth illustrating how a "standard" search engine works.

The Boolean approach to information retrieval is the most widely used. Links to documents are returned only if they contain exactly the same words as your query. Even if a site is related in some way, it would never be retrieved unless it contains the user's search string. In order to get better results from this, most search engines finesse things a little. The results from the inverted file are modified by factors such as: where the search term appears in the item—whether the string of characters appears in specially tagged areas such as titles and heads or appears early in the body text of the HTML document; how close the search words are to one another, or whether they form an "exact phrase"; the frequency of occurrence of search terms in the inverted file; whether the search terms appear as keywords in the metatags in the HTML file's head; and how frequently the terms appear in relation to the document's length (greater frequency indicating a probable greater relevance). These techniques gradually move over into semantic analysis—for instance, selection by the frequency of occurrence of words with heavier weight given to very uncommon words. (This is probably slightly unnecessary, as their occurrence in the inverted file, coupled with their realisation in the search term, is already "unusual" enough.)

The two key methods of semantic analysis of the web are hier-archical—based on ordered word relationships defined by a data-base—or self-organising—based on the buildup of evidence of search strings finding their correlates in practice.

The simplest method of constructing a semantic network is to use a precodified arrangement of terms and their correlates. A docu-ment can be used like an expanded thesaurus, widening and clari-fying search possibilities[29] by aiding query formulation through synonym relations between words and hierarchical and other rela-tions between concepts. Whilst top-down, "hard" semantic net-works come into being on the basis of automatic word-sense disambiguation—the syntactical machine that allows and disallows conjugation with what word, with what it 'means'—they aggravate polysemy in the sense that all "dictionaries advertise semantic dis-crepancies,"[30] which allow other diachronic and synchronic mean-ings, other takes to leak through. However, hard semantic networks are like dictionaries again in that even if effectively and constantly enriched by lexicographers, they still only really com-pose logs of past significance.

At the same time, whilst their hierarchical organisation allows for an extremely coherent co-ordination of words from a single per-spective, they are unable to negotiate the variable status of words as they are used. Allegory, irony, metaphor, repurposing—the rich meshwork of language that mitigates against its petrification—all go like woodcutters amongst the trees in the database, whilst utterly incommensurable figurations of language such as sacred-ness throw up errors, not just of computation, but of the essence they pretend to.

One way of attempting to avoid disjuncture between the semantic model of the information referenced by the search engine and that of its users, in the way commonly imposed by hierarchically organ-ised systems, is to assume that the words that are most commonly found together are actually related in some way. This is a technique that makes best use of machine rather than human interpretation of data. In Latent Semantic Indexing,[31] a set of documents is represented by a matrix whose entries are measures of frequencies of occurrences of terms in each document. The greater the frequency of co-occurrence, the greater the relevance. This matrix is then approximated by a sum of rank-one matrices determined using a singular value or related decomposition. This allows for great compression of the data and fast, relatively robust and encompassing referencing of sites.

However, what is found to be most related in terms of quantity doesn't necessarily match for each user, or each search. Latent Semantic Indexing finds a way of working the inverted file—mined with homonyms, synonyms, and routes to a thousand pointless choice trees—that plays to the data-processing strengths of computers and thus avoids the implicitly ontological nature of directories. However, these techniques are always caught in a self-organised conformism to the homeostatic pressures of what is statistically deemed, by frequency of use and by frequency of co-occurrence, to be the most relevant.

Searching for the most relevant, the most related—simply rendered as the most linked-to—is another technique adopted by a variety of search engines in compiling their results from the inverted field. AltaVista, Excite, Infoseek, and Inktomi[32] rate sites higher in their list of search results if a substantial number of sites link to it. Google, usefully, makes this process visible and useable, allowing backlinking from its results. Related to "citation analysis"—the scheme whereby the relative importance of scientific papers is determined by the frequency of their being cited by other scientific papers—is another approach adopted in different ways both by the Web Stalker[33] and by the "Clever"[34] project at IBM: "We have developed a new kind of search engine that exploits one of the web's most valuable resources—its myriad hyperlinks. By analysing these connections, our system automatically locates two types of pages: authorities and hubs. The former are deemed to be the best sources of information on a particular topic; the latter are collections of links to those locations."[35] "Authorities" are sites that are linked to many times; "hubs" are sites that contain many links.[36]

Despite IBM's claims, Clever has no way of actually defining a topic other than by resorting to imposing hierarchical taxonomies. What it does do is—by defining a limited set of properties (links-to and links-from, as a way of organising an interpretation of the topological form of the web)—use some of the ways the web is actually put together to develop a representation of the emergent, unpredictable interplay of multipolar gravitational tendencies within the hyperlinked structure of the web. Some of these may be sufficiently closely clustered to be interpretable from specific perspectives as a topic. Other sites which might be highly pertinent from other perspectives might not link at all. What Clever has usefully done, though, is to distinguish the structure of the web from its content and use it as an organisational principle. What they collapse in their descriptions of the project is the distinction between the hierarchical pretence to objectivity and what they actually represent, which is an aggregate of subjective decisions by the thousands of people making sites to incorporate hyperlinks. Here, "objectivity is less about realism than it is about intersubjectivity."[37] "Self-organisation" as a phrase may smell like anarchist democratics, but it is in the choice of which elements register as the evidence for, or as the most consequential part of, the self-organisation of this data that the political choice—closed to scrutiny or reinvention—as to what is important on the web or about the web is made. It is a symptom of a self-reinforcing "misplaced concreteness" that the mode of interpretation of processes becomes the means by which they are molded.

Go to a search engine of either sort and type in "Jamaica." You"ll get information on holidays coming up first—along with banner adverts for Sandals resorts. Type in "Africa" and you'll get predominantly wildlife and famine. Self-organisation of data is organised on the basis of what "self" is determined to be important. This, at present, is something put into place by the demographics of internet use. How data is interpreted and processed, how the grammar sorts and orders the strings of symbols (whether they are hierarchically ordered, or ordered according to emergent compositions of specified elements), has immense importance. When most of this work is done by a closed culture of proprietary specialists, finding ways in which this process can be opened up to speculation and organisation by other forms of "self" becomes even more imperative—finding ways in which this process can be opened up to speculation and organisation by other forms of "self" even more so.

BLAH, CLICK, BLAH, CLICK, BLAH

During the first batch of journalistic excitement over the web as a phenomenon, there were many articles of the "around the world in sixty minutes" variety. Someone sits at their desktop and links their way round the web. Despite the tenuous relation of geography to the act of calling up HTML files on a computer, it did speak of the enthusiasm generated by a device that could incorporate the most distant elements within one interface. Most of these articles were written at a time when there were no search engines (the only things that came close at this stage were lists of ordered and annotated links) so the "travel" had to be done by connecting from one site to another by links that had been constructed on a site-by-site basis. The fascination generated was that, solely by virtue of this meshwork of links, and even in the early stages of this technology, a path could be constructed through extremely distant resources. The distance in this case was supplied by geography.

The distance that now provides the most amazement is that of subjectivity. ASCII is text in its mobile form. The standardised procedure of writing as a sequence of claim–argument–conclusion becomes extraordinarily distributed, messed-with. The consequentiality of sequence becomes, not unimportant, but subject to a richer field of influence. This offer of surprise or detail or resource, this at least potential richness, produces the condition of the link, how it is arrived at, what it articulates.

SAFEWAYS

Establishing gateways between different elements of networks is an essential part of communications practice. From the development of interactive interfaces to mainframes, to the subnetwork of Interface Message Processor nodes that enabled the establishment of ARPANET, and on to the creation of every hard and soft device and protocol, the history of network computing is that of increasing the circle of inclusion of hardware, software, and datatypes. How that connection is managed, what protocols channel it, are the focus of antagonism in debates that see themselves as being primarily technically oriented. However, although the crucible that these conflicts come to heat in is that of technics, they are doped with many other traces. What interfaces allow, what they bring to bear, what elements they move into proximity or remove from the chance of coming into composition, what assumptions they make about the formations that move through and with them, what patternings they imprint into the way in which things are ordered or establish terms of composition—all exist and establish conditions at the logical, semantic, syntactic, social, economic, aesthetic, and political levels.

Just as, within an economy organised increasingly not around objects but processes, and within a logistical context of just-in-time delivery, the gateway to the factory is where much of the inward and outward processing of information and materials is now done; or where the interface to companies has been stripped down to a telephone number connected to a database by a voice (a voice that, even though itself coming into being through a stripping away of commerce from the street, will become increasingly redundant as sales carried over automated networks increase), the point of access becomes crucial on the nets.

Search engines work on the basis that they can turn any site into something only one click away from their search results, almost a subsidiary section of themselves. The development of portal sites is a way of turning the internet from a distributed network into a centralised one. Hierarchies such as the Domain Name System (DNS), or its categorical inverse on Usenet, were relatively late in interpolating the meshwork, allowing every object on the net to have a unique address accessible from a central root-node. Node power is intensified the higher you climb. This remains practical and unproblematic, so long as the system is open, with location and structure visible and interrogable, at every point. However, there is an increased tendency for the visibility to be locked up. (On a small though crucial scale, some shows of net-based art have blocked the display of URLs from the link status messages at the bottom of the browser window and in the location bar. On a larger scale, though, compelled by the same drive to increase dependency of users on portals, browsers are being developed that tie in to specific search engines and built-in results to enquiries on "key" topics.) Equally there is the potential, once the industry "matures" with the formation of effective cartels, for limits to be placed on the speed of accurate linkage to maintain multiple returns to the portal within one search session.

The possibility of capture of such root nodes becomes not just a matter of control but, on a temporary basis, also one of decontrol. Slipping the wrong signal into the centre of a hub—such as when, in early July 1999, Ivan Novkovic famously spiked TV coverage of the Germany vs. Yugoslavia football match with a call for demonstrations against Milosevic in his home town of Leskovac—offers immense possibilities for cutting away the appearance of order.

At the same time, it is pretty much the same tactic used by sites that spam search engines to climb up result hierarchies by including reams of invisible keywords, or have multiple editions of a site with different metatags and spam content.

NETWORK OF STOPPAGES

Control over the way in which links occur, the way in which they are interpreted, has become a key issue for web design. A list of suggested ways for sites to use links echoes the approach that is becoming widespread:

> Guidelines for effective linking:
> ~ Links cannot create content, but they can ruin it.
> ~ Links should reinforce your message, not replace it.
> ~ Most links should point into your site, not away from it.
> ~ Most links should appear as footnotes, away from the main text.
> ~ Links to outside sites should open a new browser window.

~ Every link is a maintenance issue; link sparingly if at all.[38]

Each web site is to become its own portal, feeding only into its own. Every site an intranet. Whilst on the web we are urged at once that "Everything must be published!" any form of external conjunction must be done with immense prophylactic care. (The Clever project's mapping of clusters of pro-abortion and anti-abortion web sites showing their close interrelation and extremely rare cross-linking provides a good example of this.)

Of course this reads as pretty much the exact inverse of most attempts to invest links on the web with various kinds of poetics. Read this list of rules through again, but kind of backwards. Make a web site that does exactly the opposite of what the list instructs—top art, mate. Guaranteed.

It is at the same time the very limited nature of the link within Hypertext Transfer Protocol that makes both takes on its use possible. The link in normal use is extremely narrow in terms of the information it allows about itself or in the transition from one anchor to another. This allows the actuation of a link to result in either a surprising conjunction or one that is completely expected. A link in a web site places it in a material—not automatically allusive, or even referential—conjunctive relation to other documents on the web. Steven Johnson sharply places its particular role: "The link is the first significant new form of punctuation to emerge in centuries."[39] Being—within HTTP, at least—simply a form of punctuation frees the link up from some of the portentous baggage strapped to it.

Much has been expounded on the basic theme of hypertextual linkages as at once a form of augmentation of text and of readerly poaching of inventive power over the text. However, it is clear that the technology has additional possibilities. Rather than hypertextual ceding of control to the reader, there is the chance to establish the power of contextualisation, the power to follow and establish in advance any argument or use of the text that strays—to establish that the author has already "gathered" that these allusions or threads of argument could be made. No association by the reader need worry about going unprecedented within the matrix of this neurotic urge to completion. It is clear from the gluttonous expansivity of the leavings of some writers on the web that hypertext can become as richly detailed and engulfing as Piranesi's fantasy prisons.

However, if we start with an acknowledgement of the simple way in which links are formed and the very restricted nature of their movement from one anchor to another, rather than an imposition of a literarily inspired compulsion to recapitulate particular models of thought as fact, things have the chance to free up a little. In most browsers there is a popup menu which allows links or other resources to be opened, saved, forwarded, and so on. This itself is a start at making some form of expanded range of modes of use available—including expanded terms of readership, composition, reuse, and storage familiar from hypertextual theory. Whilst links are only one of the range of objects that the menu operates on, it might be possible, for instance, to expand this range of uses to include some expanded sense of what links might be.

Presently, though, what the above list of constraints on "good" linking suggests is that the degree to which meaning can be attached to or implemented by a link—at its simple level of conjunctive punctuation—how much it brings together, to what extent it veers towards fragmentary "disassociation" or togetherness between both anchors, depends on the degree of framing of the link. The link works along a continuum of expectation from shock to the already anticipated. This continuum is drawn along the line of indexicality.

The common use of frames to index sites perhaps sits at one end of the paradigm, with every subsequent link being kept within the tutelage of the primary indexical frameset. Somewhere near is the indexical link from a to b, internally within documents, or to external sources. These unilateral associations, however, immediately become complicated when there is a difference in any of the various ways the sites are formulated. This can be in terms of design, of technical level (which browsers or plug-ins they demand), on ideological grounds, or at least on grounds of public appearance. For instance, the politely racist conservative Southern League provides, for the benefit of users linking from the openly neo-nazi Stormfront, a disclaimer of its white suprematism in favour of just wanting things the way God ordained down South. You can see something similar in terms of rhetorical 'scale' when cozy simple home pages—showing pictures of a family's house, the people in the house, and snaps of what they look like and like doing—include portentous links to "the search engines we recommend."

There are links operating on the basis of providing routes through sites; hypertextual uses of links based on allusion or the choice of progressive pathways through multilinear narratives; malign links; antagonistic links; supportive links; links between peer sites; links to gain status by association; psychopathic links— you can be anything, the link could be to everywhere; links traded between sites solely to boost the appearance of advertising revenue in annual reports. All of these are, because of the limited nature of the link, based on a dialogue between the interpretation of the two conjoined elements.

These are rather "hot" uses of the link, though. Their use may equally be blasé, shut off. The relatively withdrawn process of the search hijacked by Natural Selection is just as much run on indifference—in the same way that link actuation is a quick way of avoiding downloading immense GIFs or applets. One use of links that acknowledges this, but also punningly overcomes it, is the use of links to create innuendo. (Steven Johnson describes this particularly well with regard to early versions of the web site Suck.com, which was made up of allusive, condensed prose riddled with links.) The perpetually tripped-up slapstick of meaning also forms the basis by which much of the work in Natural Selection operates.[40] Somewhere further towards the latter along the expectation–surprise continuum, it works on an aesthetic of addition, the piling-up of multiple threads of implication, double-entendre, and self-undercutting that forces the user, if they can be bothered, not into a smooth plateau of inference and lovingly fondled argument iterated in abundance, but something thicker, something more prone to blow off its head whilst attempting to shoot itself in the foot.[41]

INFORMATION TRANSFERENCE INTERRUPTED

Earlier, it was suggested that using software, or types of use of software, or modes of searches, could be developed as a form of exploratory laboratory illness. Freud invented the term "transference" to describe the displacement of affect from a repressed condition onto the artificial figure of the analyst. This was a synthetic stress produced as a means to operate at a more abstract level on the underlying problem. "The transference thus creates an intermediate region from illness to real life through which the transition from one to the other is made. The new condition has taken over all the features of the illness; but it represents an artificial illness which is at every point accessible to our intervention."[42] As a technique it encourages the same investment of emotion and involvement that allowed Joseph Weizenbaum's program ELIZA,[43] a sentence-generator that famously mimicked the responses of a nondirectional psychotherapist, to convince users that they were undergoing an initial psychiatric interview.

Transference is marked by an absence. It can be a substitute for an experience, a "something" that cannot be expressed, that blocks comprehension. The analyst investigates what is inexpressible—allows a latent conflict to become a current one under experimental control that can be interrogated. This, in its "positive" form, is the very "unsayable" living truth, for him definitive of the human, that Weizenbaum later mobilises against instrumental reason, the mental strictures of a technocracy which claims that "the only reason we have not yet succeeded in formalising every aspect of the real world is that we have been lacking a sufficiently powerful logical calculus."[44] But there is a circularity to this problem, this "ineffable"—that is to say, utterly ideological—quality of humanity also moves in the opposite direction as the very means of locking people into instrumental patterns: rules, habits, obedience.

A recursive phenomenon, transference was the mechanism by which Freud hoped to make a science of psychoanalysis.[45] At the same time, the possibility of effecting transference was reliant on the authority vested in psychoanalysis under the sign of Science. ELIZA's ability to effect transference to itself equally relied on the idea that it was " . . . clothed in the magic mantle of Science, and all of Science's well-known powers may be attributed to it."[46] Once properly in the hands of the analyst, whose attention and favour are so much desired, the supposed difference between ordinary suggestion and analytic suggestion is the calculable and controllable nature of the latter. The patient can be induced, by its virtue, to specify their desire by exact phrase, by name of person, to constrain within certain languages or dates, to search only for certain pre-ordained datatypes, to associate from any of the specified words. The pen on the pad turns the dial of the mental radio being tuned back in to the Voice of Oedipus.

Whilst the analyst is therefore supposed to be able to remain outside the scene that such a role creates, using this device in order to deny and ward off the fragmentary and incomprehensible fullness of the world through an identification with the Master, with the Law. His brain is become as an interview room. A single bulb shines down on two chairs across a bite-marked table.

As Freud acknowledges in "Analysis Terminable and Interminable," transference was an idealisation, a fictional tool that provided a way of working through messy life. It is the resistances, skids of meaning, clarifications, pun-loops that provide transference with its opening chance, but also its interminability, that we can take as something more, as the material for composition.

Information transference here becomes a kind of laboratory sickness in which conceptual, disciplinary, juridical, cultural, political, and other "norms" or expectations of meaning and linkage—the switch-tongue bound, made orderly—can also be adopted.

Each search, but also each piece of software, can usefully be approached as a transferral, a synthetic agglomeration of knowing, sensing, and doing. When you drive a car your mind fills out to the space occupied by the vehicle. You sense its shape in order to manoeuvre safely, or however. Equally, conceptual proprioception can be elaborated in order to negotiate the multiple levels of meaning-making in a search. The user mobilises and becomes infested with, composed through, flocks of sensoria, a billion symptoms, neurosis at the service of knowledge, or a simple slimy crawl of the switch-tongue at the point of slipping away into babble and the learning of language.

NOTES

1. http://www.mongrelx.org/Project/Natural/index.html

2. There are also archives of sections of the net. The search engine DejaNews began an archive of all Usenet posts going back to its inception in 1979. This archive was subsequently taken on by Google.

3. See info on the Echelon system at http://caq.com/CAQ/CAQBackIssues.htm

4. This project, coordinated for Mongrel by Harwood and Matthew Fuller, essentially presents itself as a straight search engine. However, when any of several thousand words that are directly racist or have racialised connotations are entered as search strings, the Natural Selection search engine returns results that, while innocent-looking, drop the user into one of the over thirty other sites on and off the mongrel domain. Collaborators in producing the work include: Hakim Bey, Byju, Critical Art Ensemble, Stewart Home and Daniel Waugh, Mervin Jarman, Richard Pierre-Davis, Dimela Yekwai.

5. http://www.mongrelx.org/Project/Natural/BAA/heathrow/index.html, a site produced by Mervin Jarman.

6. http://www.mongrelx.org/Project/Natural/Venus/, a site produced in collaboration with Dimela Yekwai.

7. Claude E. Shannon, "A Mathematical Theory of Communication," *The Bell System Technical Journal,* Vol. 27, pp. 379–423, 1948.

8. Sigmund Freud, "Transference," *Introductory Lectures on Psychoanalysis,* the Penguin Freud Library, Vol 1, Angela Richards and James Strachey, eds. (London: Penguin, 1991), p. 482.

9. G. L. J. Chaitin, *Algorithmic Information Theory* (Cambridge University Press, 1987).

10. Mark Poster, *The Second Media Age* (Cambridge: Polity Press, 1995), p. 86.

11. The Temple of Confessions web site is at http://www.sfgate.com/foundry/pochanostra.html.

12. Guillermo Gómez-Peña, interviewed by Mildred Thompson in Glenn Hapcott, ed., *Interventions and Provocations* (New York: State University of New York Press, 1998), p. 6.

13. McSpotlight's (http://www.mcspotlight.org) most successful element was its use of frames to directly comment on the official McDonald's web site. Irational (http://www.irational.org), renegade Teletubbies fans, and other groups such as the Barbie Liberation Front produced ostensibly "real" sites on behalf of the companies and culture products they loved the most. Whilst even honest-to-goodness fan sites are often forced to mark themselves as "unofficial," some catalogue sites have been known to stage "hacks" of themselves in an effort to gain press coverage.

14. Guy Debord, "Report on the Construction of Situations and on the International Situationist Tendency's Conditions of Organisation and Action," in Ken Knabb, ed., *Situationist International Anthology* (Berkeley: Bureau of Public Secrets, 1989), p. 17.

15. Donna Haraway, *Modest_Witness@Second_Millenium. FemaleMan©_Meets_OncoMouse* (London: Routledge, 1997), p.199.

16. Debord, op. cit., p. 23.

17. Haraway, op. cit., p. 3.

18. Situationist International, "Preliminary Problems in Constructing a Situation," in Ken Knabb, ed., *Situationist International Anthology* (Berkeley: Bureau of Public Secrets, 1989).

19. Ibid.

20. Ibid.

21. The couple who have become charmed suitors in the institionalised narrative of "electronic art."

22. Haraway, op. cit., p. 199.

23. Frederick W. Lancaster, *Indexing and Abstracting in Theory and Practice,* Second Edition (London Library Association, 1998), p. 313.

24. Tim Berners-Lee, "www: Past, Present and Future," *Computer 29*, October 1996, vol. 29, no. 10, pp. 69–77.

25. Michel Foucault, *The Archaeology of Knowledge* (London: Tavistock, 1972), p. 62.

26. See "A Means of Mutation, Notes on I/O/D 4: The Web Stalker."

27. Donald McKenzie, *Negotiating Arithmetic, Constructing Proof: The Sociology of Mathematics and Information Technology, Social Studies of Science 23*, 1993, p. 56. A related study, on the impact of the military adoption of specific software engineering methods—in this case, the mathematically derived "formal" method as opposed to more "intuitive" engineering-based approaches—and the resulting changes in organisation, division of labour, documentation, and other wider changes resulting from the adoption of a new standard, is: Margaret Tierney, "The Evolution of Def Stan 00-55 and 00-56: A Socio-History of a Design Standard for Safety-Critical Software," in Paul Quintas, ed., *Social Dimensions of Systems Engineering: People, Processes, Policies and Software Development* (Hemel Hempstead: Ellis Horwood. 1993), pp. 111–134.

28. McKenzie, op. cit., p. 57.

29. Visual Thesaurus, a good example of a visualisation of this process, can be seen in all its ludicrously rigid beauty at http://www.thinkmap.com. This project is an interface to the WordNet lexical database at http://www.cogsci.princeton.edu/~wn/. WordNet operates basically by constructing hierarchically ordered sets of synonyms. See Christiane Fellbaum, ed., *WordNet: An Electronic Lexical Database* (MIT Press, 1998).

30. Walter J. Ong, *Orality and Literacy, the Technologizing of the Word* (London: Routledge, 1982), p. 46.

31. On Latent Semantic Indexing, see: http://superbook.bellcore.com/~remde/lsi/

32. http://www.searchenginewatch.com—a recommended site for a basic introduction to search engines.

33. http://bak.spc.org/iod. The Web Stalker, by contrast, avoids these problems by its representation of the network as a flat aggregate of links and nodes composing itself on the screen rather than

retranslating it into an ordered list. The Web Stalker does not assign importance or greater degree of relevance to sites, merely relaying the greater number of links to them by increasing luminosity of the node. Clever is far more sophisticated in terms of its mapping, however, simply by the analytical tools it is able to bring to bear on the information.

34. http://www.almaden.ibm.com/cs/k53/clever.html

35. "Hypersearching the Web: The Clever Project," *Scientific American,* June 1999. See also http://www.sciam.com/1999/0699issue/0699raghavan.html.

36. J. Kleinberg, "Authoritative Sources in a Hyperlinked Environment," *Proceedings of the ACM–SIAM Symposium on Discrete Algorithms,* 1998.

37. Haraway, op. cit., p. 198.

38. Patrick J. Lynch and Sarah Horton, "Imprudent Linking Leaves a Tangled Web," *Computer,* July 1997, Vol. 30, No. 7, pp. 115–117.

39. Steven Johnson, *Interface Culture: How New Technology Transforms the Way We Create and Communicate* (San Francisco: HarperEdge, 1997), p. 110.

40. See the work of Critical Art Ensemble (http://www.mongrelx.org/Project/Natural/Biotech/), or Stewart Home and Daniel Waugh (http://www.mongrelx.org/Project/Natural/Skrewed/).

41. See, for instance, http://www.mongrelx.org/Project/Natural/NSA/ or http://www.mongrelx.org/Project/Natural/Agent/.

42. Sigmund Freud, "Remembering, Repeating and Working Through," *The Complete Psychological Works of Sigmund Freud,* ed. James Strachey, vol. 11, p. 155.

43. Weizenbaum, op. cit.

44. John McCarthy, cited in Weizenbaum, *Computer Power and Human Reason: From Judgement to Calculation* (London: Pelican, 1984), p. 203.

45. Isabelle Stengers, "Black Boxes, or Psychoanalysis a Science?" in *Power and Invention: Situating Science* (Minneapolis: University of Minnesota Press, 1997).

46. Weizenbaum, op. cit., p. 191.

THE IMPOSSIBILITY OF INTERFACE

The graphic user interface, it is said, allowed computational power to leap from relatively isolated positions—for example, from expertly attended payroll-management machines used in the cores of banks—into new forms of relation with people and other processes. It thereby established a direct and hence ever-so-useful involvement with every part of life.

What are the terms of this interrelation, and what do software interfaces have in common with other forms of interface? A working definition is provided by Brenda Laurel. "An interface is a contact surface. It reflects the physical properties of the interactors, the functions to be performed, and the balance of power and control."[1]

Using this definition to help develop the above questions, I want to run a consideration of interface through a speculative typology of modes of interface which goes as follows:

~ Interface as distributed throughout and indivisible from the system it is part of.

~ Interface as monitoring and control of a reductive, indexical map of separate elements that can be changed from state to state, but not altered.

~ Interface as an associational structure that allows a user to manipulate, alter, destroy, and multiply processes and objects from which it is independent.

SOFTWARE: INFORMATION AND MATTER

What I am suggesting here is not simply a ladder of abstraction, but more a recognition of processes becoming internal to the computer. This is an extension of what Katherine Hayles suggests when she names virtuality as "the cultural perception that material objects are interpenetrated by information patterns."[2]

We must note that the recognition and interpretation of such patterns is itself the performance of a device—'information'—that has certain effects, tending towards the manufacture of a caesura between matter and information. This is always only the effects of an interpretative operation on matter, rather than something 'given freely.' Matter is understood to be always informational, but never pure. If matter is never simply informational we must also flip the pairing. If we are to understand informational patterns as always having a materiality, then the interpenetration of informational patterns by other informational patterns is what is discussed here as software. Such informational patterns are always understood to be embedded and manifested in materiality—the architecture of a computer, for instance.

METAPHOR

First we need to briefly touch upon metaphor. The assumption here is that metaphors will be gradually erased from mass-use interfaces.[3] Metaphors, it is typically explained, are useful in generating a way for users to imaginally map out in advance what functional capacity a device has by reference to a pre-existing apparatus.[4] However, as functionality outstrips the explanatory capacity of reference to previous media forms, this initial usefulness will diminish. The uneven spread of metaphor-reliant constructs within most applications would tend to support this thesis. Software will need to be seen to do what it does, not do what something else does.

At the same time, as in the case of animation or multimedia applications using the model of a "set," with "lighting," or the "darkroom" metaphor of Photoshop, they do remain as imaginal regimes structurating particular kinds of software.

Two uses of the magnifying glass as metaphor are interesting in this respect. In the Mac OS's Sherlock, a search tool, clicking on a button with a picture of a magnifying glass actuates a search for a string of characters typed into an adjacent field. In programs like Photoshop or Quark XPress, the magnifying glass works to perform a jump-cut which magnifies or demagnifies a selected element of the "canvas" or "page" (via either a marquee or simple click whose degree of magnification or demagnification may be set in advance via a tool settings dialogue window).

In the case of Sherlock,[5] on the other hand, the result of clicking on the magnifying glass is a list of files in which the requested string occurs. Instead of a mimicking of the capacity of sight, or of the action of lenses, what emerges is a database form: the index. (Such an asymmetry between metaphor and function is incidentally illustrative of the medial incompatibility that faces the construction of image databases.) Perhaps the designers of the interface mistook what they must have taken to be the cuteness of the name of the device for its actual function, or were channelled into keeping a metaphor ticking long after its initial imaginal power had been shed. Perhaps a "realistic" image of a syringe or a violin, Sherlock Holmes's actual technics of associationality, were beyond them?

What this suggests is that it is those elements within the wider field of software that are working to the strictures of the version economy—in which a release is demanded every six to twelve months—that are going to maintain metaphor, or have any need to do so. Such a repetition is necessary in order to keep the mass scale of users, by means of an apparent familiarity, on the upgrade path to perfection. At the same time, such programs develop interfaces and functionality that increasingly replicate those they supposedly compete against in order to make it easier for users to transfer their loyalty from one to the other.

For the purposes of this text, then, metaphor is to be understood simply as a variant of action upon an object or process, and not as something inherently necessary to interface design, no matter how useful it is or has been in generating an imaginal space for certain forms of interface. That is, metaphor takes a known set of properties and behaviours from one domain—optics or fiction in the case of the magnifying glass—and transfers them to that of the computer as an explanatory or structurating device. With every interface metaphor, there is a point at which its explanatory or structure-providing advantages collapse in the face of the capacity for mutation in the universal machine, the computer, and what it connects to. At the same time, as will be seen later in the consideration of games, there are conditions in which it is precisely this artificiality, and in their use as exploratory imaginal devices, that they have their uses.

I THOUGHT I WAS SEEING CONVICTS

I Thought I Was Seeing Convicts[6] is a documentary, largely composed of "found' material," by the filmmaker Harun Farocki. Much of the footage is of the insides of a California state prison, Corcoran.[7] Cut in with images and sound from the place, and with a prison staff training video, are short sequences of computer interfaces.

The footage from Corcoran surrounds a court case from the end of the nineties in which prison guards were alleged to have set up fights between members of rival gangs within the prison's exercise yards. As with most U.S. prisons, inmates organise themselves into gangs based on outside loyalties and racial and regional groupings. Introducing a prisoner from one gang into a yard being used by members of another produces a conflict over territory. For the guards, this is a reproduction of gangs' conflicts with each other rather than the authorities. It also condemns participating inmates to further convictions. (This is crucial under the "three strikes" system, which can be leveraged to start a prisoner off with a sentence for a small charge and, via a series of staged incidents, leave them as permanent residents and sources of budget for staff and facilities.)

Watching the yard by video, and from watchtowers, guards bet on the outcome of fights they set up in this way. At other times they "break up" the resulting fights by shooting the unarmed people involved.

This video installation is crawling with interfaces. What implications does it have for them?

I. INTERFACE AS DISTRIBUTED THROUGHOUT AND INDIVISIBLE

The particular interface I am interested in here is that put in place in the architectonics of the exercise yards, and the cameras and procedures used to control and to execute the men in them. The user is a prison officer, or a command structure of prison officers. The shape of the yard is like a slice of cake, a segment. At the apex of the segment is a video camera. Watching the feed from the camera is a guard.

If we are to take Laurel's definition of an interface as "a contact surface [that] reflects the physical properties of the interactors, the functions to be performed, and the balance of power and control," we are in a quandary. Where is the interface? In the architecture, the shape of the yard that perfectly matches the area viewed by the camera? In the shape of the lens, its refractive capacity? The circuits that turn the light from the lens into a series of pixels? The slow scan of the stored video images? The height and relative scalability of the wall? The colour of the walls? The minds of the prisoners? The regulations ostensibly governing the behaviour of the guards? The range and calibre of the guns used to kill unarmed prisoners? The skills used to stage a fight and select a target? The relations between prisoners? The records kept on prisoners and groups of prisoners? The multiple capitalist and racist mechanisms in which the prison is embedded and which it, as an industry, depends upon and reproduces? The legal system? The system of property? The idea of an individual subject accorded rights? The "three strikes" process? The protocols of wounding, honour, loyalty, and fighting within the racialised gang-system of the prison culture?

We cannot here consider the interface between guards and prisoners to be solely representational in the way that a standard computer desktop is sometimes understood to be. The interfaces here operate in many ways, through multiple procedures. Whilst the system they instantiate is fundamentally hierarchical, they also operate by means of networks of mutually reinforcing patterns, ideology, structure, and material. What the notion of interface allows us to do here is analyse how they link, how one process passes from the domain of one axiom into another, how processes are reconfigured, stripped down, simplified or made amorphous from their passage from one medial, architectural, racial, juridical regime to another. It is a particular pathway through these that the guards were able to "hack" in order to realise a level of brutality that could not be officially countenanced, or even acknowledged as having happened.

The events at Corcoran stage in effect the transition that Gilles Deleuze[8] notes when he talks about a shift from a disciplinary society[9]—which operates by confinement and naming—to a society of control—in which behaviour is modulated, as often as not using the even older device of free will, rather than molded. This modulation is ongoing, processual—a process of relational development rather than fixedness. In a sense, what is discussed here in terms of interface is how—even in the archetypal domain of disciplinary power, the prison—these two modes of power combine, how they stack up and combine, and how one mode can assume dominance over the other.

At the same time, it forces us to reject any accounts of interface as being solely or primarily to do with representation, about the manipulation of elements that are separate from the structure of the surface layer. Interfaces code in advance how and when something occurs, but cannot necessarily determine it. (It is always in negotiation with another part of the system—CPU resources, for instance.) The vectors that connect one thing to another, an instruction to an object, a node to another, a layer to a filter, are always political at the same time as they are technical and aesthetic.

To describe a structure such as a prison as a series of interfaces risks flattering the libido of the prison. It becomes something separable, the discharge of a series of pre-ordained functions, a rational, managerial process ordained by science. Discipline as a "mold" allows the interface to remain something discrete, neutral. Control as a process of constant "modulation" is that neutrality gone mobile, that soaks into everything, but that chops and swerves, demanding constant renewal of adherence to codes and processes. This is what the guards were able to manipulate, the interface between discipline, in its predictability, and the vapourous insinuations of control.

At their Palo Alto Research Centre, Xerox once staged a well-known experiment with the tagging and positioning of workers in a type-two interface. Co-workers and managers, as they moved around the building in the course of a day, had the ability to find anyone they were looking for, what they were working on, what telephone or other address they could be reached at, and their availability for communication for various levels in the hierarchy. This is typical of a control interface, but not appropriate for the class of worker that is allowed to experiment upon itself, and the system was soon dropped.

II. INTERFACE AS MONITORING AND CONTROL OF A REDUCTIVE, INDEXICAL MAP OF SEPARATE ELEMENTS

Alongside the footage of the prison, Farocki cuts in, on the two screens the interface plays on, material from other kinds of control systems. One piece of software is a schematic rendering of a building's floor-plan. It allows an operator to switch lights on and off and to open and lock doors by clicking on symbols embedded in the schematic. Other footage shows a stock recognition system built into some kind of surveillance device. The main window on the screen is a video feed from a camera following someone in a supermarket. As the shopper picks up and examines articles from the shelves, a series of pop-up menus allows the operator to specify and record the items that the target touches.

Richard Sennnett describes an interface of this sort in a Boston bakery. A "user-friendly" interface had been installed at the front end of a baking system to allow workers to control bread production without the need to deal directly with the raw materials, to make judgements about the readiness or consistency of dough, to shape loaves, and so on. The machinery allows flexible specialisation rather than mass production. The work is done by a transient force of part-timers or temporary workers supervised by one fore-

man. It is deskilled; operating the system demands pressing but-
tons on a screen, and

> monitoring the entire process via on-screen icons which
> depict, for instance, images of bread colour derived from
> data about the temperature and baking times of the ovens;
> few bakers actually see the loaves of bread that they make.
> Their working screens are organised in the familiar
> Windows way; in one, icons for many more different kinds
> of bread appear than had been prepared in the past—
> Russian, Italian, French loaves all possible by touching the
> screen.[10]

The interface, however, doesn't match up to the baking process
every time. Much of the product is wasted when the actual tem-
perature, the rising of the loaves, or some other factor fails to
match the representation on screen. There is a skip outside full of
burnt loaves, victims of automated friendly fire. Workers controlling the process via the interface have no need for an understanding of how to bake bread. The process is illegible to them.

Whilst the interface is extremely easy to use, its relation to the
procedure it manages is flawed. The monitoring and control of the
baking process is not deep or detailed enough to allow this.
Additionally, the "sociotechnical" and economic arrangements of
the bakery rely on having a workforce with no actual baking
skills—this would increase costs.

Sennett describes "alienation" experienced by an older generation of bakers as "the unhappy disassociated consciousness which
reveals . . . things as they are and where a person stands."[11] By contrast, "flexibility creates distinctions between surface and depth;
those who are flexibility's less powerful subjects are forced to
remain on the surface."[12]

The closing of doors and switching of lights on and off shown
in Farocki's film is very similar. Elsewhere, security guards working twelve-hour shifts at minimum wages—watching monitors,
wiping bar codes, checking faces—have the same relationship to
the processes they control, and those that shape their jobs, as the
push-button bakers. Like call-centre workers working with menus,

forms, databases, and series of written scripts for their speech, plus a time-per-call quota, the task is to be an interface, a stratum. As with Laurel's description of interface, this is a surface that is thick, that bristles with connections, blockages and channels, variable speeds, timeframes, and routines.

Performing a surface, manufacturing an alienated interface, double consciousness,[13] is an essential capacity of life in the "mode of information."[14] We must create faces, bubbles, blips, strings of delay, backchannels, and sabotage in the domain of work. This, rather than submerging into the well-bloodied trap of "realising our full potential" in the terms of a rigged productivity. Therefore, whenever an interface promises to make something "clear" or speaks of allowing something to work in just the simplest way possible, it must first of all be assaulted with questions, yawns, and scripts rather than rewarded with immediate identification.

It is this gap between a model of function and its actuation that in some cases describes a degree of freedom, and that in others puts into place a paralysing incapacity to act. It would not, for instance, be over-welcome in the steering system of a plane. The politics of the indexical map is produced precisely in its power to command an isomorphic relation between itself and what it controls. It must not, it cannot, slip . . .

III. INTERFACE AS INDEPENDENT ASSOCIATIONAL STRUCTURE

Only at this point does an interface explicitly correspond to the logical processes of a computer: to write, store, delete, read, and calculate on the basis of these functions. It must be added, of course, that the interface of the third kind is never, of necessity, permanently "independent" of those elements that it provides an associational mechanism for. It may, of course, given an appropriate level of access, be rewritten.

In order to develop a provisional understanding of this type of interface, I want to approach it through video games. Steven Poole's book *Trigger Happy*[15] provides a good starting point for understanding the dynamics of interface and what might be a kinaesthetics of information. One of the key themes in the book is how interaction is enhanced by the internal data-structures of the game, the models it has to govern the motion and behaviour of objects, vehicles, and bodies within the game, and how they behave on screen in relation to the user-inputs.

> Writing a racing game, for instance . . . the car can be defined as a certain mass resting, through a suspension system, on four wheels, which have a certain frictional relationship with the road. From this very simple mathematical definition, it turns out that that "realistic" car behaviour, such as oversteer and understeer, load-shifting and tilting, come for free.[16]

What *Trigger Happy* shows here is that the simple application of Newtonian physics—acceleration, gravity, inertia, and so on, rather than a "full" model of the material world—creates a small set of axioms that combine to give a rich array of play interactions. Indeed Newton gets dropped swiftly enough when a little mutation makes for more exciting game-play or opportunity for a cartoon-style plasmatic world. Just as the "realistic" movement and handling of a car is gained by the mutual interplay of various mathematical models of certain aspects of the mechanics of a moving car, in other games very simple behavioural codes—such as when to bob up and down from behind a crate during a firefight (any amount of shooters), or when to flee a room when a leader figure is shot down (Halo)—are also derived "for free"[17] by the interplay of simple software agents governing dominant or recessive simulations of "emotion" and behaviour in non-player characters.

Much of this useful book is an extended consideration of how the axioms of games contribute to a multiple self-enframing that is either compelling (because of the richness of variations to be brought about by the combination of their various types of capacity) or enjoyable for simplicity coupled with combinatorial unpredictability.

The sweetest pleasure in many games is their coherent range of dynamic properties and the interplay between them. This is something relatively independent of processor power—think of Pong or Tetris—and extends to the ergonomic and audio qualities of a game as well as the visual. Current game platforms allow thousands of tiny variables to be computed on the fly according to complicated interactions of multiply intersecting numerical models. Early video games, and those still played on a Game Boy or on emulators such as MAME, kept such computations down to a minimum. What is important for Poole is that they are an always-consistent set of properties. Thus, what he calls their "realism" is not predicated on their being "authentic" but on internal consistency. The axioms can be codes, rather than what we understand as natural "laws"; whether these correspond to those experienced outside of the screen or are of a completely novel kind made possible by computerised media is immaterial.

Such insights into games compare interestingly with one of the classic rubrics of user-centred design, found exemplarily in the work of Donald Norman. The focus should be on "interacting with the task, not with the computer." In a video game, the task is precisely to perform the interaction with the computer, for as long as it remains pleasurable or compulsive. (It is this blurring of the focus of interaction, where one interacts and works within patterns of information, folded into further patterns, embedded in matter, that allows for actual abstractions such as the concept of "immaterial labour.")

Potentially, at least, the standard grammatical positions of subject and object which work-oriented usability theory is predicated upon become caught up in arrays of dynamics that are processual rather than fixed and concerned with the interplay of freedoms and constraints rather than outcomes. So it is easy to imagine that we leave matter behind.

However, a reading of video games shows that the best of them—and there are plenty which simply translate the tiresomeness of work—still have a concept of task, which is now this very processuality, built in. There, the pleasures of the game become those of multiple virtualities. This is a virtuality as becoming and as involvement, a link between Hayles's use of the term and that of Deleuze, who says, "What we call virtual is not something that

lacks reality but something that is engaged in a process of actualisation following the plane that gives it its particular reality."[18]

Such pleasure is found in how games borrow or, by virtue of
interaction, differ from the codes of other formations: film, in
terms of the phenomenological and informational capacities of different "camera" angles, pace, lighting, and framing conventions in
various kinds of game; simple narrative modes, such as quests, folk
tales, whodunits, and multi-choice gamebooks, in how they differ
from them in terms of the linear irreversibility of the sequences
and the granularity of action; the potential mix of visual codes,
photorealism, Albertian perspective, animé-style deformation, etc.;
how stylisation, reaction, timing, and patterning are transducted
from different sports, plots, weapons, and vehicles, and bring with
them gender codes, bodily capacities, different kinds of action
amplification and kinetic fluidity, one-game-only finger skills built
into muscle-memory, informational stamina, how the interplay of
different codes can be thought and sensed into. This "realism" is
also what is gross about many games, gross in the refusal to stage
these conventions as axioms, as synthetic.

Now, however, we can return to Norman's formulation of a
good interface. The task to be operated on is now to be operated in:
patterns of information operating on other patterns of information.
The task is to reformulate the task, to be coupled to that process,
to be absorbed. At the same time, the position of the interface-
designer needs to be blown open. Norman is right when he com-
ments that "every interface designer is also a system designer," that
"nothing can be designed in isolation."[19] However, there is within
interface design a tendency to close down what counts as an element within a system. It is an insight, but not sufficient, to establish that a designer of a computer system needs to make sure that
it is capable of being cabled up to the other electronic media systems the user might have. We need an understanding of systems
that never stop in their unravelling and invention of new connections.

Neither, however, should connections, combinations of
things—things are always combinations—be welcomed simply on
the basis of their hybridity. Paul N. Edwards describes a presenta-

tion of a computer game with an output beyond peripherals that might "intuitively" need to be connected:

> As we rode the eye of the bomb to the white flash of impact, we experienced at once the elation of technological power, the impotence and voyeurism of the passive TV audience, and the blurring of the boundaries between "intelligent" weapon and political will.[20]

This hybrid is recounted as Edwards describes General Norman Schwarzkopf or some other walking abscess playing video with the bombing of Baghdad in 1991. Although this sentence might overestimate the case for the existence of political "will" as a form of individuated intentionality rather than the playing-out of drives and capacities built into various mutually stimulating formations and dynamics, it does show that the interplay of certain medial, computational, erotic, political, and material arrangements are inherently part of a "system" that is ostensibly only technical. How such combinations are forged, how they proceed, their constitutive axioms and protocols, need necessarily to be taken up in a consideration of interface.

The massive gallimaufry that is Microsoft Word has been discussed elsewhere,[21] but it is perhaps useful to compare these kinds of programs, the applications that fill the hard drives of most computers, with the kind of cultures of interface that Poole discusses in *Trigger Happy*. One distinction is between simulations and games devoted to play:

> Simulation . . . promotes in certain genres (driving, flight, games) the primacy of supposed "realism" over instant fun. A true video game deliberately simplifies any given situation (imaginary or real) down to its essential, kinetic parts.[22]

Such applications simulate, for example, a writing machine, a perfection for a certain sort of textual production, modelled by systems designers whose conception of writing is formed by the boundaries of the workplace. This is not to say that they form a coherent whole that is ever embodied in even one place of writing (indeed some of their elements are of fundamental operative and conceptual difference) but that the composite writing-system[23] they embody is that composed in the conjunction of the series "writing" with the series "work." It is the clutter of "realistic" models of writing or other processes, which at the same time hide their acculturation, that Word and related programs insist upon that makes them close to simulation games.

At the same time, all of computing rests upon simulation at the most fundamental level—for instance, the simulation of CMYK on RGB screens. What is suggested here is that those simulations are not universally navigable in the same way, and as a result, need to be made in a way that is interrogable. Here we can take something up from Poole's implicit suggestion that a more enthralling game is one which connects the user immediately at a deeper level with the underlying axioms of the game—software that reveals its processes as it enacts them.

THE ONE INSIDE THE OTHER

The three types of interface suggested here can clearly also be seen to operate one inside the other at different moments. When you use a WYSIWYG (What You See Is What You Get) interface in a Desktop Publishing program, you operate on an interface of the second kind, using the conventions of the third kind. There is a reference to an object, the document.

The process is also reversed in programs such as those which allow the automated monitoring of employees by keystroke surveillance or web-logging—an example of the second type—built into word-processing or web-access software—an example of the third. One must be clear that this is not simply something reserved for work subordinates (although it is more likely to be applied the more mechanical the demands of work are) but something unleashed at the outset by automation. At another location, at another speed, within the layers of capital's transduction of skill, one could imagine a program for building up data for the use of expert trading systems operating by secretly monitoring the buying and selling patterns of stock market traders.

The scale or detailing of references to an object is another axis of difference. One distinction between the first and third mode of interface is that once an interface becomes entirely digital, there is no room for a vague action. Comparing the use of computers by artists and designers, one research group notes that there is a reluctance to use computers in the initial stages of a work.[24] Computers do not usually provide for good initial sketches. Boolean logic ties any interface action into a yes or no, where any mark into data is as fixed as any other element. Equally, every object or element of data in a file, once it has been saved from the buffer, has the same status. No matter how many layers are assigned to it, the undo function operates in linear time.

In the theory of information and control systems, primarily using interfaces of the second kind, there is a distinction between first- and second-order control. In the first case the control of a "steady-state" of a process is given over entirely to a mechanism—a thermostat, for instance. Second-order control is where the operator provides an overview of these processes, interprets and recognises patterns, and is able to react rapidly to them.[25]

One model of the "human data processor" echoes this distinction in the way in which it produces a division of labour between mental processes, a "cooperation between a high-capacity parallel-processing system that functions subconsciously, and a sequential conscious processor of limited capacity. The sub-conscious processor takes care of routine tasks, and only in unfamiliar environments and tasks is there a need for higher-level control of the processing by the versatile, but slow, sequential processor."[26]

Thus, the models of discipline and control are recapitulated at the structural level of the interface and of the subject modelled by it. However, as we have seen, once control folds in upon control, messes with its too-easy seriality, opens it to inspection, blocks, breaks, scratches, and streams, there is perhaps the opportunity for something else to emerge.

DESIGN: THERE ARE PEOPLE CONNECTED TO THIS
COMPUTER. IT WILL SHUT DOWN IN _10_ MINUTES

Typical in user-centred design research is the statement to test-users trying out a prototype of a new piece of software: "I'm testing the product; I'm not testing you."

Typical of statements for the back blurb of third-party application manuals is, "Need to learn Blah Blah Version Blech Fast? This is the book for you."

Whilst the usability researchers depend for the effectiveness of their research on generating an environment of trust between themselves and the test user, once the software is inserted into a work environment users will specifically be tested against how they match up against the software. The cruelty in this relation is a direct inverse of the institutional niceness of the usability test. The more that is invested in making the software user-friendly, the more employer, co-workers, and technical staff are justified in demeaning the worker who has not internalised its regime. Research based on making software achieve fitness to desired task is as much about enhancing productivity and regimes of work as it is about the pleasurability of a tool fitted perfectly to its purpose.

It is not, therefore, simply a question of expertly making a tool most fit for its purpose. Rather, we might begin by tracking the various mutations of the series, axioms, drives, enframements, formations, and so on that a work brings together and finding ways of staging that combination without blocking out the conceptual and material potential for recombination in different forms, or any access to them by others.

What follows is to understand that "output" can only ever be a provisional term. For the contexts in which most software is used—work—the question, "What does the user need to get out of this?"—as if users were agents that only come into composition with the software of their own volition—is infinitely loaded. Following this, "whole tasks" that can be measured and designed through at every stage to increase or improve their performability, pleasure, coherence, comprehensibility, and function only ever exist temporarily. Even when the apparatus for their execution is designed, manufactured, and distributed in the millions, the task whose execution they embody may change or disappear. The devices will be erased or recombined, part used, bastardised. It is ensuring functional openness to this bastardisation which needs to be a primary task of software interface design.

THERE IS NO CALCULUS OF BECOMING

What remains if we are to take such a discussion of interface seriously is to ask how this process, rather than a "position," of interface design can itself be opened up?

The poet Jackson Mac Low had it this way. The poet is "preeminently the maker of the plot, the framework—not necessarily of everything that takes place within that framework . . . creates a *situation* wherein he invites other persons and the world in general to be co-creators with him! He does not wish to be a dictator but a loyal co-initiator within the free society of equals which he hopes his work will bring about."[27]

Mac Low, in almost classical statement of the "open work"[28] policy of some of the later twentieth-century avant garde, clearly knew what was at stake in the capacity of poetry to generate actual freedoms of perception and language, and—relevant to computational culture—the non-determinate processes of chance often built into his work. At the same time, the claims for the poet as a stable position, as master of signification, the situation*ist*, which might be read into such a passage need themselves to be thrown over to the same processes.

Franco Berardi ("Bifo"), in an early text on computer-based media, states, "Whenever a social universe forms adequate to the technological and communications potential of actual social brainpower, we call it Renaissance."[29]

There is something necessarily circular about Bifo's formulation here in that it describes a process that is continually catching up and changing the entities that compose it. When the poetics of creation in Mac Low's terms expand to generate an unfolding of their full social, aesthetic, and technical capacity for resonance, such a moment creates an explosion. Such an explosion can take place at many levels of scale: the molar politics of class or individual; a flowering coalition of insight, rhythm, and sensation familiar, but not often enough, to culture; it can take place in software and by means of software or in those moments where absolutely nothing is left untouched.

In most cases it is, along with the workers in the bakery described by Richard Sennett, entirely sensible to answer interface with utter indifference. There is so much boredom, structural cruelty, and stupidity governing the physical properties of the interactors, the functions to be performed, and the balances of power and control they perform and embody. The slow deliberate violence of the state burying its hatred for life inside the body of a living prisoner—a relation embodied in the apparatus directly surrounding them, the buildings in which they are fixed, and the society that provides their cloak—is one example of interface, is one which can only be met adequately with its destruction.

But in other moments and dynamics of interface, it is this unleashing of patterns of potentiality and innovation that Berardi calls a renaissance (which sometimes comes as revolution, and other times as the simply careful and persistent attention to opening up a particular range of possibilities by virtue of "recombinant intelligence"[30]—intelligence that realises its own multiple virtuality) that is at stake in what has momentarily settled up as interface. And it is by what it combines with, where it goes, what it makes happen, that we will know whether it itself is worth anything more than the usual indifference.

NOTES

1. Brenda Laurel, ed., *The Art of Human–Computer Interface Design* (Reading, MA: Addison Wesley, 1990), p. xii. Laurel uses this definition of interface in a context where she is describing two kinds of doors: one that allows ingress and egress by both sides by means of a handle—the normal internal door—and another installed at a secure government site in which face and name had to be given in order to gain entry via a door with no handle.

This definition of interface is used for its relative precision. Other, equally influential, definitions of the term can be found which encompass a more substantial set of arrangements and processes. For instance, Jef Raskin suggests that interface is "the way you accomplish tasks with a product—what you do and how it responds—that's the interface." *The Humane Interface: New Directions for Designing Interactive Systems* (Reading, MA: Addision Wesley, 2000), p. 2.

For two useful texts on doors that explore in detail some of the micropolitical arrangements they embody, and which are suggested in brief by Laurel, see Bruno Latour, "Where Are the Missing Masses? A Sociology of a Few Mundane Artifacts" in W. E. Bijker and J. Law, eds., *Shaping Technology/Building Society* (Cambridge, MA: MIT Press, 1992), and "The Berlin Key, or How to Do Words with Things," in P. M. Graves-Brown, ed., *Matter, Materiality and Modern Culture* (London: Routledge, 2000).

2. N. Katherine Hayles, "The Condition of Virtuality," in Jeffrey Masten, Peter Stalleybrass, Nancy Vickers, eds., *Language Machines: Technologies of Literary and Cultural Production* (London: Routledge, 1997), p. 183.

3. The argument is very well developed in Dona Gertner and Jakob Nielsen, "The Anti-Mac Interface."

4. The classic text on metaphor, which influenced much of the use of this type of device in computer interface, is Lakoff & Johnson, *Metaphors We Live By* (University of Chicago Press, 1980).

5. The version referred to here is Version 2, first shipped with Mac OS 9.0.

6. Harun Farocki, *I Thought I Was Seeing Convicts* (2000), two-channel video installation. Two texts by Farocki covering related areas are "American Framing: Notes for a Film about Malls" and "Controlling Observation," both in Harun Farocki, *Nachdruck/Imprint. Texte/Writings,* (New York and Berlin: Lukas and Sternberg and Vorwerk 8, 2001).

7. The Corcoran prison website, displaying about as much information as a children's trading card, is at http://www.cdc.state.ca.us/facility/instcor.htm. References to this series of episodes can be found at http://www.sonomacountyfreep-

ress.org/police/corcoran.html. Some of the footage is at http://www.cnnsf.com/newsvault/media/abusemov.ram and http://www.web.amnesty.org/ai.nsf/index/AMR510982000.

In an enquiry, the guards said to be running the "gladiator" fights were declared innocent. Subsequently, on November 10, 1998, the California Deptartment of Corrections made an out-of-court payment of $825,000 to the parents of Preston Tate, a prisoner killed in such combats. In a scene included in Farocki's installation, he was shot dead by a guard whilst being attacked by another prisoner. Subsequent to this and other episodes, water cannon have been installed in the yards.

8. Gilles Deleuze, "Postscript on Control Societies," in *Negotiations*, trans. Martin Joughin (Columbia University Press, 1995).

9. In a number of early books, Foucault proceeds through a series of case studies of different disciplinary formations which establish the usefulness of this term: *Discipline and Punish, The Birth of the Clinic, Madness and Civilization*, etc.

10. Richard Sennett, *The Corrosion of Character: The Personal Consequences of Work in the New Capitalism* (New York: W. W. Norton, 1998), p. 68.

11. Ibid, p. 70.

12. Ibid, p. 75.

13. For an extended discussion, see "Criminal Minded," and an application in relation to search engines in "Break the Law of Information." Following the Critical Art Ensemble's useful theorisation of the DataBody in *The Electronic Disturbance,* one website offers to manufacture elements of a bogus DataBody "Tracenoizer—disinformation on demand" (2001) at http://www.tracenoizer.org/

14. Mark Poster, *The Second Media Age* (Cambridge, U.K.: Polity Press, 1995).

15. Steven Poole, *Trigger Happy: The Inner Life of Video Games* (London: Fourth Estate, 2000).

16. A number of hacks of video games take advantage of precisely this; for instance, Jean Leandre's "retroYou r/c" (1999), downloadable at http://www.retroyou.org; JODI's "Untitled Game"

at http://untitled-game.org/; and various work by Nullpointer at http://www.nullpointer.org/. Much of this kind of work exists outside of "art" frames of reference, often only being explicable to those who have spent time developing their familiarity with the underlying structure and potentials of such programs. To spend time in such a context is, however, very rich in the way it allows the sheer artificiality of software to become known, and then to become something that revels in its own deranging plasticity.

Console games point to such currents within computer-game culture, but cannot but fail to match them. The facility to choose "Moon Physics" in "Tony Hawk's Pro Skater 3" (Activision, 2001) merely gives you a slightly looser version of earth gravity. The "expert" culture of cheats built into games which give the player everlasting armour or guns, perfect balance, and so on illustrates how much playing with the different combinations of axioms available in a game lies at the root of their fascination.

17. Poole, op. cit., p. 116.

18. Gilles Deleuze, *Pure Immanence: Essays on a Life,* trans. Anne Boyman (New York: Zone Books, 2001), p. 31.

19. Brenda Laurel, op. cit.

20. Paul N. Edwards, "Cyberpunks in Cyberspace: The Politics of Subjectivity in the Computer Age," in Susan Leigh Star, ed., *The Cultures of Computing* (Oxford: Blackwell, 1995), p. 75.

21. See "It Looks Like You're Writing a Letter: Microsoft Word."

22. Poole, op. cit., p. 41.

23. Friedrich Kittler, *Discourse Networks 1800/1900,* trans. Michael Metteer with Chris Cullens (Stanford University Press, 1990).

24. Colin Beardon, Sue Gollifer, Christopher Rose, and Suzette Worden, "Computer Use by Artists and Designers: Some Perspectives on Two Design Traditions" in Morten Kyng and Lars Mathiassen, eds., *Computers and Design in Context* (Cambridge, MA: MIT Press, Cambridge, 1997), pp. 27–49.

25. For example, L. Hirshhorn, *Beyond Mechanisation* (Cambridge, MA: MIT Press, 1984).

26. Jens Rasmussen, "The Human as a Systems Component," in H. T. Smith and T. R. G. Green, eds., *Human Interaction with Computers* (London: Academic Press, 1980), p. 70.

27. Jackson Mac Low, cited in Jerome Rothenberg, *Revolution of the Word: a new gathering of American avant-garde poetry, 1914-1945* (Boston: Exact Change, 2000).

28. See, for example, Umberto Eco, *The Open Work,* trans. Anna Cancogni (Cambridge, MA: Harvard University Press, 1989).

29. Franco Berardi (Bifo), *Sand in the Mouth,* trans. Paula Casanova, *Semiotext(e),* Vol. 4, No. 3, 1984, p. 25.

30. Franco Berardi (Bifo), *La fabbrica dell'infelicità. New economy e movimento del cognitariato* (Rome: Derive Approdi, 2001).

THE LONG, DARK
PHONE-IN OF THE SOUL

In Los Angeles they are collapsing in the streets. Down at the stock exchange, brains are melting. More is happening than anyone can possibly cope with. Information overload—the very contemporary scourge.

Possibly the most abundant and competitive life-form in this apocalyptic effusion of detail: factoids. Shake a media executive for an opinion, and along with his wallet and dandruff you're likely to get: "A typical issue of the *Los Angeles Times* contains more information than a seventeenthth-century Englishman was exposed to in his entire life."[1] Notwithstanding the fatuous unprovability of such an assertion, it is one that resonates with a general apprehension. Rather than being faced with a qualitative improvement in intelligence, the human race is doomed to fry under the sheer quantitative increase of infotainment to be processed. In an information economy in which anxious formats format an anxious reality, there is a handy answer being proffered. For delicate sensibilities exhausted by mental stimulation, intelligent agents are hailed as just as sure a tool for coping with the spew as a machine gun is for doing business with a banker.[2]

Independent software agents that roam the nets; crawlers; ultra-personalised data-services from the aggressive to the ambient; insidious taxonomies sheathed in unctuous butlers or data-santas with the tastes of a magpie and jammy hearts of gold. But before we get into the technical specifications . . .

THE INTENSIVE CARE OF THE SELF

A moist, warm little homunculus of tender flesh, sheathed in thick sweet mucus, is clamped down hard into layers and layers of bone, bone which can—under the correct conditions of clemency and etiquette—be progressively stripped off to reveal the true being. As the bone and metal casing folds down, resplendent in the force of its sovereign originality, a purple clot of compressed flesh cowers naked, yearning for an intimacy that it can never accommodate. In its skull-bunker air is changed every two seconds. A thick purple umbilical cord trails slackly down into its spine. In the windowless white-tiled production areas which have airlocks and are kept at a constant thirty-seven degrees centigrade by a coddling system equivalent to 9200 hostess trolleys, the human is panicked at being "misrepresented" by its agents. Its heart, opened to the page on the account book where all the frauds and tenderness are stored, reads:

"The world outside is strange, complicated and incoherent."

This delicate clot of feeling is dropped like a fish into fat. Into a new room. A capsule with flickering walls. It opens its eyes and sees a bewildering collage of images each in its own window: flowers, details of European cathedrals and Shinto temples, Chinese landscape art, magnified images of insects and pollen grains, many-armed Indian goddesses, planets and moons of the solar system, abstract patterns from the Islamic world, graphs of mathematical equations, head shots of models male and female.[3] The rapidly accreted symbology of cyberspace pastorale: great lurid globs of data, sphinxes thrown up by mist; bit-mapped epiphanies; time-lapse video of colourful diseases; insurgencies mapped into larva-lamp belches, then wire-framed; the very miserable zentertainment.

Intelligent agents form around a compound of three usages of "intelligence": that of facts or news that are discovered, and perhaps made commerce of; that connoting an individual mental understanding, here perhaps more closely as a quality that can be scientifically measured (if not quite put into operation) as IQ; and finally, the definition offered by James DerDerian in looking at the field of International Relations: "Intelligence is the continuation of war by the clandestine interference of one power into the affairs of another power."[4]

The development of intelligent agents is also, at the same time, the development of those destined to use them. From this neat little loop, ramifications multiply out into the production, distribution, and formatting of intelligence. The human frame, once feared incapable of being hurled along in an automobile at an immense thirty miles per hour, is now assailed by a tripartite hurricane of bits. Intelligence as object, intelligence as suppleness or technique, and intelligence as war.

The point of intersection of all these spiralling formulations is subjectivity.

For the user, the services of agents are invoked to give you the information that you need, to give you the information you don't ordinarily have time to find, and to have it given when you need it, in a manner that suits your humour. Whilst for the agent, if the user is "a man of the least spirit he will have fifty deviations from a straight line to make with this or that party as he goes along, which he can no ways avoid,"[5] the agent is also to take these breaks, shudders, deviations, and insolubles and reconcile them into a recognisable whole.

Such a mix of behaviours corresponds to the first two definitions of intelligence: that of intelligence about an object or fact, and that of intelligence as measurable quality or technique. This modulation of two patterns—those of the agent and the user—into one could perhaps be said to produce a gestalt, a third mind that is the recording sum of the development and changes in the patterns as they move through time. However, this gestalt is not just one of harmonious synthesis but also the point of leakage—one that is directly implicated in intelligence as war—that pulls things out of equilibrium and into the realms of meaning-making apparatus and power.

One response is to take a step back from this cacophonous danger and reformulate the relationship.

For the user, the agent can function as a kind of sympathetic magic. Purify the self by its endless bespoke repetition. A way of finding an other that will be always self-similar. This is the escape from information-overload through the construction of safe worlds. Just as Hilton or McDonald's is a place you can go and always find the authorised version of America, this is an escape from history into cyclical time.

Here the agent, potential vector of not just communication but transformation, becomes another tagging device in the social prison. The tag locks you into one place and stops you moving. The agent roams the nets to return with a mirror. Stay where you are. Don't move. Hooked up as a device for the reiteration of the One, narcissus becomes narcosis.

Attempting to maintain and pursue only its own interest, and therefore bypass alienation, the loop between agent and user rapidly contracts into nothing. For, if "self-consciousness exists in and for itself when, and by the fact, that it so exists for another; that is it exists only in being acknowledged,"[6] the master is always dependent on receiving the gaze of the bondsman, who, in a reflex of liquid termination, absorbs the One and winks out of existence.

FROM OBLITERATION THROUGH PURITY, BACKZOOM

Formulated somewhere in the tension between the regurgitated alienation epiphany of the doom-gurus and a legitimate technical problem, the following scene:

Almost entrepreneurial, almost newly gut-bucketed, not so much dressed down as dressed across (so great is their will to communicate). The heroically swivel-chair-bound cosmonauts of inner space. Optic nerves toasting in the light of reports back from the front. Reports of superhuman passions and superhuman perversities. File-transfer debauches perpetrated without enthusiasm and without hope. This is not so much a scenario of the agent being a fragment of ego, detached and flung out into the world to forage for glory, so much as the ego as glutinous aggregate that forms in the place of a common-sense compromise between ideal and possibility.

In the same way that Lyndon B. Johnson, on ascending to the White House after Kennedy's brief and brutal reign, insisted on having all of his phone calls tapped, agents can provide a strictly empirical answer to the matinee rescreens of the eternal questions: What am I and what the fuck am I doing here? This is the problematic formed in the tension between formatted information and formatted data-personality: the version of the user stored in the agent's database.

(How long before an exciting hospital drama features an attempt to restore personality to a post-traumatic amnesiac by what emerges as stored in their databases?)

Autonomous software agents make choices and execute actions on behalf of the user. They embody the expertise to find and present information to the user, respond dynamically to the user's changing goals, preferences, learning style, and knowledge. In many contexts, this implies the ability to find or create alternate representations of information. Autonomy requires some degree of intelligence in the agent, and, given the current state of artificial intelligence, of pre-existing structure in the underlying information.

The other bottleneck is formulated well by Jaron Lanier: "I am concerned that people will gradually, and perhaps not even consciously, adjust their lives to make agents appear smart. If an agent seems smart, it might really mean that people have dumbed themselves down to make their lives more easily representable by the agents' simple database design."[7]

Fragments are added to the spew as a consequence of what? Public relations? Debt? The ingestion of substances? A capsized mind? Tight shoes? Philately? The occurrence of both of these bottlenecks is rooted in the transition of something ostensibly more messy into something conforming to database needs. Both multiplied and perplexed, the Bakhtinian version of dialogue as the word as two-sided act is subject to an uncanny mutational turbulence wherein machine hermeneutics meets vivisection. Acted upon by the labelling, classification, positioning, and fixing routines of databases, perception becomes rooted to observable stimulus-events which can be manipulated and—hooked up into a polygraph of inhibitory and excitatory interactions—correlated (correctly or incorrectly) to the internal events of the user, database, or agent. Thus, between and within the continuing onrush of the spew; the databases formatting the spew and making it readable to agents; the interpretative interaction of the agents and databases; the interaction between agent and user—whereby both are read and reformatted; and the messy transformational behaviour of the user on behalf of which the agent is making choices and executing actions, there is a possibility for the development of a plurality that can resist anything better than its own diversity. This possibility, however, is the point at which intelligence as technique and suppleness segues into intelligence as war.

Currently, as Lanier points out, the fog of intelligence is thinned by the depletion of possibility. Just as users of PDAs are forced to turn their script into that of pre-schoolers in order to make use of their machines (writing-recognition programs training the user to write in a way it can recognise); or just as some live their lives to avoid producing data that might arouse the suspicions of credit agencies; and—conversely—just as insurance ratings are made on the basis of data-mined assessments of residential area, sex, age, trade, and other details, the existence of a person in dataspace, their data-body, has often become more important than their flesh. This organic residue of citizenship, gathered into the fold of insurance, banking, medical services, and product preferences, is gradually reduced to a device for the registration of punishment for transgression of, or reward for compliance to, these structures.

At the same time that software packages such as Textract are developed to cross-reference and search every possible kind of database for the purposes of centralised agencies like the police and the military (including video and audio surveillance footage; supposedly safe data-sources such as medical, employment, and school records; as well as more obviously open sources such as credit ratings, tax, and criminal records), network technologies are impacting on vertical control. The Los Angeles Police Department caused a sensation amongst officers when it introduced a career-tracking system that included the use of neural networks to spot patterns of types of disciplinary infractions that might lead to dangerous, unauthorised behaviour.[8] Whilst data-mining has been used by astronomers to map new galaxies, it is also being used to bring a flat, scrutinising light to every kind of darkness. That these pattern-finding technologies are of a kindred technical nature to agents and the databases that they negotiate illustrates that pattern-enforcing and pattern-producing are also not exactly distantly related.

That this personalised inquisition may well have the bludgeoning sophistication and accuracy of customer profile questionnaires is perhaps a relief, for the moment. However, it also provides an opportunity for some commentators to suggest that this software needs to use some kind of personality as its interface to increase the user's fun and productivity quotients. As promoted by boom gurus, the anthropomorphisation and personalisation of agents is developed to encourage an engagement with "intuitive" narratives and the suspension of disbelief through projection onto and through the agent. Personalities are intended to communicate the agent's predispositions to users, thereby enabling them to understand, predict the results of, and successfully deploy the associated behaviours. Librarians, butlers, and well-trained and faithful dogs, as well as the familiar noir image of the detective as a maverick thought—a stray neural impulse in some great night-time brain—have all been suggested as models.

Whilst experts from industries such as theatre and animation have offered themselves as authorities in the humanities (the study of what humans can be reduced to) in order to supply the amount of remorselessly cheerful or focus-grouped cantankerous-but-cute necessary to make this technology a real hit, we are perhaps first more likely to see the introduction of branded personalities for knowbots. After all, who wants to know what they themselves might be interested in when they can delve into the media subconscious of a star selling diagrammatics of their personal or projected tastes—along with the inevitable myriad of nested brand-endorsements and links? Who can wait till Martha Stewart becomes a fully automated choice machine?

Before Artificial Life labs start ratcheting up the volume and churning out a dazzlingly hi-spec array of customisable taste modes from the Epicurean to the anorexic, it might be worth considering that while many interface designers believe that users are constantly plunged into disorientation, or getting lost while attempting to find their way through myriad connecting documents and links, the truth is often rather that users are sucked into overorienting loops that are impossible to escape from. Having this trap facilitated by a clip-art personality might make it a great interpersonal experience. As you and your agent share the growing sense of imprisonment, watch its vocabulary of boredom gradually run to panic and then mysteriously dry up.

On the nets, supply exceeds demand by several orders of magnitude: spew. This has effectively meant, for instance, the demise of many but the most exclusive or well-niched subscription and pay-per-view services. Perhaps agents as devices for the production of remote and expanded demand are useful to capital because they can be seen to artificially inflate demand to match supply through the proliferation of automated hits—thus allowing the realistic possibility of widespread tariffs. If this occurs, however, it is rather likely to fail again after a time, at the key choke point to the flow—the entry to the user: the distinctly serial port of the human eye socket. In the longer term then, in order to maximise the potential for profit, there needs to be a tightening-up on supply—political and economic censorship. This, for the truly modern user, coupled with the invention of new orifices and the diversification of online time. These are not considerations specifically inherent to agents, but they do form part of the grimly crumby fitness landscapes that agents may well be run through.

Perhaps, since "Information is everywhere supposed to produce an accelerated circulation of meaning, which appreciates in value as a result of accelerated turnover,"[9] we will see the development of a new kind of internal marketplace—a competition between different agents to supply the greatest amount of information, thus increasing their importance and hold in terms of influence and attention time.

BACKZOOM: FROM SELF-ABSORBED TO SELF DISSOLVED

Hitting the floor gut-clutched by food poisoning or glue. Your brain is getting cored by the gathering knowledge that you inhabit a room fitted with five copies of you. Each performs a separate task: one whispering hawser-thick algorithms into a corner; one studying the ceiling; one doing an eight-bit beat-boxing of the aggression signalling noises of the haddock (steady and low, increasing in speed with the intensity of the situation); another flatly observing the rest to offer a caustic running commentary on what she can see them doing.

. . . from an eternal backwards compatibility as obliteration; through interaction as disciplinary body-counting; to the aggregate of agent/user subjectivity as network. Personalisation as airport transit lounge. With control configured as cost-control, the agent as preternaturally happy accomplice to automated nit-picking carried out by an immense army of minuscule pedants concerned with the functioning of virtues and vices of a perfectly healthy everyday sort, the agent as vendor of fly-specks of detail perkily brought to your attention by focus-groupings of bits, gets sliced by the rationale of the surgery of plasticity:

> Capital only retains anthropological characteristics as a symptom of underdevelopment; reformatting primate behaviour as inertia to be dissipated in self-reinforcing artificiality. Man is something for it to overcome: a problem, a drag.[10]

From the point of view of capital's rictal year zero the agent is a device for strip-mining consciousness. As models of subjectivity are increasingly produced locating it as a certain level of consistency within a network of networks, the production of devices for the integration or navigation of these networks becomes paramount. The optimum personality-profile is a compressed curve towards a blanked-out transcendence mirrored in those abattoirs of communication—internet sites that contain nothing but links. Within this terrain of interstitial blight, surfing is depth. Behind the alluring promise of cascades of deleted idle time being efficiently suffused with a sense of meaning and significance, intelligence as technique becomes a factory of fact. Programming is here not something that merely occurs to a material substrate (either the chip or the human), but that recomposes it in an obliteration that aims for the sublime, that ends up as permanent fascist spasm. Bite down on this. Here come the electrons.

At the other end of the continuum from narcissistic disappearance. At the widest point of the backzoom. With the megamachine integrated to sub-atomic level. The user becomes the motor output for the laughter of control.

Stepping aside from this well-prepared transition from lockdown to vaporisation,[11] we can move into something else: the composition within conflict of intelligence. Writing about the different, mainly English, writings that emerged from experiences of prisoners of war and concentration camp internees during and after the Second World War, Ken Worpole notes: " . . . two class definitions of 'freedom' that are in complete opposition: In one it is a quality associated with splendid isolation; in another it is associated with the communality of things and the mutual aid of interlocking relationships."[12]

These constructions of freedom—the first that of the officer class, the second developed in the ranks—bear an uncanny resemblance to the direction of much of the debate around the political and cultural meaning of the nets. In a novel bearing directly on the war but suggesting the consequences of an alternative outcome, Philip K. Dick has one character, Frank Frink, ponder his use of the Confucian interface to the future, the I Ching. An oracle whose counsel could be "brought forth by the passive chance workings of the vegetable stalks. Random, and yet rooted in the moment in which he lived, in which his life was bound up with all the other lives and particles in the universe."[13]

Without wishing to engage in considerations of the actual use of this device (which has corollaries in the Tarot, tea-leaves, and coin-tossing as a way of informing or computing, of making judgements or of throwing another view into a situation, and thus blocking, channelling, or producing energy), it is to the politically charged thick connnectionism apparent from these two quotes that we can look for material and perhaps unexpected development in the construction and usage of agents.

A first clue to this might come from a look at one of the technologies offering potential in the development of agents.

A neural net acts as an associative memory that stores links between inputs and outputs, stimuli and responses. Neural nets are believed to offer a topological parallel to models of some aspects of human brain function, such as associative pairing and generalisation through similarity, but they still lag far behind the complexity of this three-pound lump of muscle: The most advanced nets have 10,000 nodes, while human brains contain over 100 billion neurons. If there were enough nodes, they could in theory be used, with varying degrees of success, to patch together a model of any system. But as there is no noticeable shortage of human beings, the replication of them or their behaviour seems somewhat unnecessary; the uses are elsewhere.

Neural networks can be used to learn the patterns resulting from the aptitudes and interests of the user. Because this learning constitutes the development of rules which can be stored, the network can also be equipped to represent to the user what it is doing as it learns. As they work through association, perhaps nets could even be used for bringing to the attention of the user, along with the daily harvest of information, some of his or her own interests, or behaviour that they might not have noticed. All this makes them a particularly suitable base technology for use in the construction of agents.

Alongside neural networks as a source for the development of agents, there is also the area of programs that launched a thousand security jobs: viruses. Before the advent of viruses it was possible to suppose that "outside the computer there is only chaos: dust and various contaminants from which this fragile universe of order and logic must be guarded if it is to continue to function."[14] For the logician, "the digital computer has this virtue: its design is perfectly logical down to the scale of electrons; it has conquered the disorder of the natural world by the hierarchical principles of symbolic logic."[15] For virus writers, the fascination that other worlds could be built up from the scale of the electron to function under the aegis of other forms of rationality has a slightly more powerful pull. The computer virus, self-replicating, moving within and between computers and files, exists in the seemingly untenable mix of ratiocination and contamination that it can make at once both fruitful and poisonous.

How do these technologies provide us with a sense of what a useful approach to agents might be? One that enriches rather than diminishes?

A completely harmless virus is an impossibility. All viruses by their mere presence on a computer can cause collateral damage, accidentally overwriting data or causing a system crash by using up memory. Their existence in obscurity; promulgation by evasiveness, and intimacy with their environment; their common combination of high technical intricacy with dumb, bravado-heavy goofy humour reveals them to be deeply connected to both intelligence as technique and as war.

Neural nets find boundaries not by the tracing of a line, but by developing a sense of what is on either side. They are more suited to producing multiple drafts of a situation than by analysing it to a summit of correctness. Whereas the virus has an infection strategy, the neural net is explicitly constructed as open to new inputs. It is in the combination of minute, pestilential intimacy and openness that suggests how agents might be developed to at once engage in the communality of things and the mutual aid of interlocking relationships and provide, through the addition of new kinds of agency, an extra degree of tangledness to it.

In this thick mess of connection permanently on, around, and within the user, where the isolation of "the self" is insufficient, we also need to find a way of disturbing the often repressive conviviality which is typified by Worpole's ideal of working-class connectivity. Here, Nick Land's suggestion of "functional connectivity from anti-productive static,"[16] the development of units of cultural mutation, confrontation, and sensory transference—allying itself with the gawky functionality sensed in the notion that desiring machines only work when they break down—provides a way to also connect with other dynamics of composition.

This is not a call for the sensibility of infinity to enter computers (which are necessarily finite structures operating within their technical constraints in a finite time), but rather a way of dealing with their finitude through connection to their pestilential quirks.

As a quasi-autonomous element composed through the structuring, application, and exploratory function of intelligence, agents have an automatic connection with the function of the intellectual. Two models which complement each other and the mix of logic and contamination of the virus alongside the open, messy functionality of the neural net, are that of the "specific intellectual" and the "dissident." The first, proposed by Michel Foucault, suggests that the intelligent agent can be used as a conduit for, and as an attentive, mobile and open translator of, information flows that can be utilised in "concrete, precise, definite terms, within a determinate situation."[17] The second, offered by Julia Kristeva, suggests that allied to this stripped-down version is a kind of awkwardness:

> It was perhaps inevitable . . . that the dissident function of the intellectual should have been asserted by the unemployed of the future, those intellectuals without a job, or students with no prospect of being taken on by any restrictive and bankrupt social "formations."[18]

If you have used an internet search engine to look for files concerning a particular topic, you will know the madness that is the result of the loss of everything but reason.[19] Everything that might possibly be connected by the use of that keyword is connected, if only momentarily, for the period of that search. This is an incompetence that encompasses, as a matter of accident, judicious competence: a totally logical correctness that is nothing if it is not also wrong. Here, where a fastidious indecisiveness forces the production of novel typologies and patterns of identification, the intelligent agent as an apparition of pure reason—a creature of code words, sets, and rigid syntax, of the assembly line along which packets of data are sorted, labelled, and processed, located in the specific context of information-flows—learns to perform its dissident function.

What is proposed then in the development of intelligent agents is the application of shitness; stupidity; surprise; the inherent, congenitally unadapted funkiness of bad code. That memory storage as deliberate anachronism—eternal backward-compatibility, even in its end-state of ultra-conservative stasis—can be interrogated and even used for its own ends, if not won over by gawkiness. That the cumulative oddness of very small sensory experiences produces a functionality of its own. And—for either user or agent—that " . . . It's better to have ten consecutive failures or insignificant results than a besotted passivity before the mechanisms of retrieval."[20]

NOTES

1. Doug Glenn, president of Mattel Media, in "Gender Blender," by Michael Meloan, *Wired,* November 1996, p. 52.

2. "Maybe some of them fancy educated fellers can out-talk poor folks like us, but if you just pull that little trigger and make some noise—why, it's as good as a college diploma!" Kate "Ma" Barker, cited in Brad Steiger, *Bizarre Crime: True Crime Tales with a Twist!* (London: Pan, 1993), p. 133.

3. Neal Stephenson, *The Diamond Age* (London: Roc, 1996), p. 475.

4. James DerDerian, *Antidiplomacy* (Oxford: Blackwell, 1992), p. 21.

5. Lawrence Sterne, *The Life and Opinions of Tristram Shandy, Gentleman* (London: Penguin, 1985), p. 64.

6. G. W. F. Hegel, *Phenomenology of Spirit* (Oxford University Press, 1979), p. 111.

7. Jaron Lanier, "My Problem with Agents," *Wired,* November, 1996, p. 43.

8. The only pattern-recognition needed to deal with the police is a sense of history: "My grandfather had to deal with the cops/my great-grandfather dealt with the cops/my great-great-grandfather

had to deal with the cops/and then my great-great-great-great . . . When's it gonna stop?" KRS One, "Sound of the Police," *Return of the Boom Bap,* Jive Records HIP 142.

9. Jean Baudrillard, "The Implosion of Meaning in the Media and the Implosion of the Social in the Masses", in *Questioning Technology,* eds. John Zerzan and Alice Carnes (Philadelphia: New Society Publishers, 1991), p. 159.

10. Nick Land, *Meltdown* (Abstract Culture No. 1, Coventry: Cybernetic Culture Research Unit, 1997), p. 6.

11. This simultaneous transition from lock-down to vaporisation, from atomising universality to minuscule particularity, perhaps also has its parallels in McLuhan's thesis that globalisation increases tribalisation.

12. Ken Worpole, *Dockers and Detectives* (London: Verso, 1983), p. 54.

13. Philip K. Dick, *The Man in the High Castle* (London: Penguin, 1988), p. 19.

14. J. David Bolter, *Turing's Man: Western Culture in the Age of the Computer* (London: Pelican, 1986), p. 74.

15. Ibid.

16. Nick Land, op. cit., p. 2.

17. Michel Foucault, *Remarks on Marx* (New York: Semiotext(e), 1991), p. 139.

18. Julia Kristeva, "A New Type of Intellectual: The Dissident," in *The Kristeva Reader,* ed. Toril Moi (Oxford: Blackwell, 1986), p. 294. She continues: "If it had not been for this situation, the Western intellectual would still have too many 'reception facilities' that allow him to feel at home, including and perhaps above all when he is 'in opposition.'"

19. Louis Aragon, citing G. K. Chesterton: "The madman is not the man who has lost his reason. The madman is the man who has lost everything but his reason." *Paris Peasant,* trans. Simon Watson Taylor (London: Picador, 1987), p. 215.

20. Félix Guattari, *Chaosophy* (New York: Semiotext(e), 1995), p. 224.

IT LOOKS LIKE YOU'RE WRITING A LETTER

MICROSOFT WORD

A recent film has one character blown to death at his keyboard. Underneath the desk is a bomb controlled by a keystroke-counter. When the number of taps on the keyboard drops below a certain rate, off goes the explosive. A real innovation in the switching system the bomb uses is that it is tied into the grammar check in Microsoft Word. The victim is unable to keep tapping away at the same key until help arrives. He has to keep composing grammatically correct sentences, line after line, despite the cramp in his fingers. Needless to say, knowing that this is both a sure wellspring of verbiage and a scriptwriter's shortcut to bathos, he composes a last letter to his loved ones. Eventually, though, the agrammaticality of emotions or of tiredness sprawls out of even these second-guessed fingertips, and as a green line appears under a patiently panicked phrase, up they go.

This lot is being written with every toolbar visible, every feature enabled. One third of the screen, a large one, is taken up with grey toolbars pocked with icons. There is a constant clatter of audio feedback clicking, shuffling, and chiming as the user's attention is pulled away from putting together a piece of writing into the manufacture of the text as a perfectly primped document. As you read, understand that these words are to appear against a background fill effect of white, grey-veined marble.

Microsoft Word is part of a larger package, Office, which contains Excel, a financial spreadsheet program; Powerpoint, the digitised answer to the glory of the overhead projector; an array of bits and bobs including low-level code generators for Visual Basic and HTML;[1] and some stunning clip-art.

If, contra McLuhan, "a society is defined by its amalgamations, not by its tools,"[2] then Office is an attempt to pre-empt this amalgamation by not only providing what rationalist programmers are content to describe merely as tools but also the paths between them, how they intermix, and the boundaries and correlations between their different functions, the objects they work on, and the users that they amalgamate with.

All word-processing programs exist in part at the threshold between the public world of the document and those of the user, the writing and what lies behind it. These worlds may be subject to: non-disclosure agreements; slow or headache-fast procedures of readying for publication; hype into new domains of intensity or dumbness; technical codes of practice or house style; the meeting or skirting round of deadlines; weedling, borrowing, speeding, or any other of the dynamics which compose themselves around putting a bunch of letters together. How does Word meet, detour, or expand these drives, norms, and codes in writing?

Like much else, word processing has escaped from its original centralised, hierarchically positioned place within large organisations and single-purpose computers.[3] It has also stayed put, shifting things about in the workplace, but also being trained there. And what it changes into at work affects how it is used, what it allows to be done, outside of work. The work of literary writing and the task of data-entry share the same conceptual and performative environment, as do the journalist and the occasional HTML-coder. The history of literacy is full of instances of technologies of writing taking themselves without consent from structures aimed at containing them—technologies which at the same time as they open things up instantiate new norms and demands, from reading the bible to completing tax statements. At each new threshold, heresy and fraud are opened up as possibilities, but at the same time are forced to operate on one more terrain at once.

Microsoft Office slots into the all-you'll-ever-need-for-the-home-office shelf in the software supermarket, with all the placing that only those who own the store can manage. There are bound to be some scintillating demographics on exactly who uses the software and how tucked into the data-storage of some go-gotten demigod somewhere on a Seattle corridor: figures laying out exactly how Microsoft projects future patterns of work and use for their software, what tools will be needed to meet the challenges of a new era of productivity or something. But these aren't the clues we have to go on. What we do have to help discover what kind of user is being imagined and put into place is the mountain of material the program presents. Since its early versions, Word has swollen like a drowned and drifting cow. The menu-bar has stretched to twelve items, the number of toolbars to eighteen. Don a white coat, open a calculator, multiply these two figures, then cube them, and you get a scientific idea of the extent of the domain which Word now covers.

According to James Gleick, features are included in Word with "little more purpose than to persuade the trade press to add one more 'Yes' to the feature-comparison charts that always accompany word-processor roundups."[4] With its roots in Taylorism, where work is divided up into discrete measured tasks carried out by a single operative, the user or worker or soldier appears to Computer–Human Interface design only as a subsystem whose efficiency and therefore profitability can be increased by better-designed tools. Whilst, according to John Hewitt, "the disappearance of the worker has, in fact, been an aspect of most design theory since Morris,"[5] what this means contemporarily is that the disappearance of the worker is best achieved by the direct subsumption of all their potentiality within the apparatus of work.

The volume of features in Word is often represented as a disastrous excess, but this is excess fitted up as standard. What draws users to the site of their own special disappearance is possibly even the contrary drive for the disappearance of work in autonomous behaviour as an ideal of free work: "We can call someone autonomous when s/he conceives and carries out a personal project whose goals s/he has invented and whose criteria for success are not socially predetermined."[6] Gorz's definition of autonomous labour provides a useable rule of thumb, a workable trope for autonomy which is conflictual and negotiated rather than its more fantastically "independent" variant. As a device it allows us to understand that a program like Word doesn't deny autonomous work or the desire for it, but parasitises it, corrals and rides it at the same time as entering into an arrangement of simultaneous recomposition of scope.

The surplus-feature mountain warehoused in your computer is stored against the possibility of your ever needing it, against the possibility of the user's self-expanding or changing purpose or datatype. Whilst any one individual or work practice may only use a very narrow selection of Word's entire capability, like all software of its kind there is a dramatic break with that area of the Taylorist model of work which involves strict division of labour in the actual form of the equipment. (This is usually achieved by system-management software and by work practices.) In comparison to the disappearable production-lined individual, here workers are expected to encompass and internalise knowledge of the entire application which replaces it and to be able to roam about, freely choosing their tools and their job. This is the quandary for the self which Foucault presents: "How does one govern oneself by performing actions in which one is oneself the object of those actions, the domain in which they are applied, the instrument to which they have recourse, and the subject which acts?"[7] But it is at once doubled for the self whose actions, object, domain, and instrument are amalgamated with a material-semiotic sensorium—a program— whose entanglements and interrelations are so multifarious. (For at least one accredited philosopher founding an enquiry into word processing the problem is far worse: "The anxiety of losing a hold on professional integrity and sinking into popular culture must be restrained for the sake of thinking out a phenomenon we are now living through and in which we are participating."[8])

The feature-mountain refutes theories of hardware determination of software at the same time that it makes a full victimising incorporation of the user into the application laughably implausible. It is again as an amalgamate—a subset of those both within and connected to the "universal machine"—that it deserves to be worked over. The threshold that it composes also incorporates, as well as the obvious economic factors, compositional articulations produced by hardware capabilities and innovation; developments in programming languages and technique, as well as those of the structuring and organisation of such work; and the propensity of digital technologies to have arranged some form of connection to the networks. All of these factors, of course, intermesh along with the various corporate instruments used to determine and decide upon their various and relative importance.

OBJECTS IN THEIR PLACE

Word is, with the rest of Office, put together using object-oriented technology. A program is made up of a set of objects—each one a unique, unchanging entity within the program, complete with definitions of data and operations which it is permitted to carry out. Objects can pass messages between one another as well as being able to make requests on other objects. Objects have a sense of how data "behaves"; therefore, each object is responsible for checking the validity and "sensibility" of the data that it is working with. As a result, programs made using this approach are generally more flexible in their ability to accommodate a variety of datatypes and processes. The inner workings of the object, and interrelations between objects, are, as with most programs, hidden from the user. However, some inkling of their function can be gathered from what is visible at the interface and in use—in the division of the tools up into toolbars and in the various ways in which tools are shown to be able or not able to work on specific pieces of data.

The relative reliability of this approach to programming makes it particularly suitable for constructing programs that are built up version by version rather than regularly rewritten. This way of handling different forms of data and activity thus has to be thoroughly coherent at all stages. Crucially for Office, this is what allows objects to be used across seemingly separate applications. The use of toolbars in Word is predetermined not only by the inherent qualities of object-oriented software, but by Microsoft's approach to using it. The productive part of the company is structured into work teams with closely defined domains of expertise and function responsible for each class of object—for instance, each toolbar. Object Orientation as a method therefore passes over into the structure of working practices, with each programmer having an equivalently limited position.

The user becomes an object, but at a peculiar position in the hierarchy of others. The user-object is excluded from the internal transmission of information, and instead allocated representations of elements of this information as interface. This information is allocated on the basis of how closely it corresponds to the "tasks" that users have come into composition with the software to perform. The screen is divided up into little counters clustered into groups, each of which is oriented to a particular task. Each task may then break down into a hierarchy of subtasks or further specifications as to the description of the task. The closed world of objects and other objects interrelated according to strict protocols is visible on screen as changes in data-state or in the mode of the program. Further interrogation of the program is denied. This is not something specific to Word, and it cannot necessarily be described as problematic, but it does point to a direction in which objects could be developed with more independence from the tasks they are locked into. For instance, there is a strict division between the program's ordering of Clip Art and Word Art. They appear at different depths in the choice hierarchy, are searchable by different means, and control computationally different forms of graphic. But crucially, whilst they are both categorised as a form of Picture there is only a limited cross-over in functions that can be applied from the toolbar of one to the object of another (i.e., the Picture toolbar can control the wrap function relevant to a Word art object but little else. Both toolbars can call up the Format Object dialogue box for an object from either. It is not possible to use the contrast and brightness controls—also a function in Format Object—that are in the picture toolbar directly on a Word Art object.) There is an assumption built into toolbars that they accomplish a certain wholeness in circumscribing the task that they construct or that is translated by them into the realm of objects.

How are the tasks and the objects that compose them ordered? Several tools are present in more than one toolbar; others can only be accessed several layers deep into menu hierarchies. For instance, Animated Text, a function which (whilst unable to be converted into a web document by saving as HTML) makes Netscape's < blink > tag look classy, allows you to add a little bit of fairyland to your text with sparkling pixels and flickering borders. In order to animate text, the user must choose Format from the menu bar, select the option to format Fonts, and then choose the Animation level from the three types of font-formatting available. To many users this option is likely to be so far down a choice tree that it drops off it completely. Its relative silliness in the context of a "serious" work application, however, makes it a good example of not only how tasks are ordered, but also—seen in the conventional attacks on Word and most recent mass-market software for being bloated with features—what is considered to be useful or gratu-itous. Font animation is not available directly from any toolbar, whilst the ability to specify the font, its point size, and whether it is bold, italic, or underlined, is deemed to be so necessary that it is included in both the "Formatting" and "Ribbon" toolbars. This has implications not only for the quality of the interface, but also for how Word is composed as an amalgamate, what forces and drives it is opened up to in order to shape its prioritisation of events, tasks, objects, datatypes, and uses.

It should be possible to analyse a piece of software on the basis of procedurally documenting every point which constitutes an event, to record the points at which we move from one state to another or at which boundaries are produced to certain behav-iours, not merely within modes but at every level of the software. Begin to extrapolate out, following through, from installation, to licensing agreement, to splash screen and on into the hierarchy of functions of the actual program. Describe at each point, at each moment that constitutes an event, how it functions as part of a series of closely interlocking fields such as processor characteris-

tics, operating systems, models of user behaviour, work organisation, qualities of certain algorithms, the relative status of various
document or file forms (for instance, the recent half-botched
attempt to incorporate HTML generation), the availability of class
libraries of already written code and more or less densely determi-
nant ones such as markets, forms of copyright, aesthetic method-
ologies or trends and so on. Equally, an application, especially one
intent on sucking all potential functions toward it, can be interrogated on the basis of those functions that are absent from it. For
instance, which models of "work" have informed Word to the
extent that the types of text management that it encompasses have
not included such simple features as automated alphabetical ordering of list items or the ability to produce combinatorial poetry as
easily as "Word Art"?

H-E-E-L-L-P

One futile place to look for answers to such enquiries would be the
various types of help that Word places at the disposal of the user.
There are five forms of help available from the application, with
Balloon Help on the Mac being perhaps the simplest. On a simple
rollover from the mouse on a menu item or interface component,
a speech-bubble appears next to the cursor giving a short description of the item's use and function. Similarly, leaving the cursor on
any of the tool icons will simply display the name of the tool. With
these two, the most useful aspects of the Word's help facilities
begin and end.

The Help menu also provides a link to launch Explorer
(whether it is specified as your preferred browser or not) to open
the advice section of Microsoft's site. The other major aspect of
Help is Microsoft Word Help. This is a simple archive of information held together by an index and hypertextual linkages between
different areas of the documentation. Whilst it is possible to find
information by browsing this resource, it largely helps to know precisely what you require help about, as the user already has to be
able to name the function in order to describe it to Help's search
facility and thus find the information. To complicate matters,
Microsoft often uses apparently "simplified" versions of generally

used words (such as "jumps" instead of hyperlinks) both instead of and alongside the more common terms. Whilst there may be a vast amount of data in the various layers of Help to edify users with a spare hour or so, it is worse than useless to users who need a particular element of information in order to allow them to achieve what they want to do straight away.

Microsoft Word Help is also where you end up if you fall for the ruse of accepting help from the Office Assistant. Rocking on its heels, whistling, getting rubik, turning into a filing cabinet, the version for Apple computers is an economically and cutely animated Mac Plus with Disney-vermin legs. Windows users get a paperclip. Rather than offer actual help, this takes the proposition of the digital assistant, the low-grade Artificial Intelligence that will in the permanently rained-off future help the user make those crucial tabulation decisions, but settles for kewtness over function. The narrow bandwidth of the solely language-based Turing test is side-stepped with animations on the assumption that if enough body-language is thrown within a rectangle of a few hundred pixels, users are going to grant it the same assumed high-informational content that they transferred to jittery CU-SeeMe pornos. This feigned step up the evolutionary ladder towards symbiotic intelligence is abandoned a couple of branches down the choice tree when the user actually tries to get help from the assistant and is dumped back in the disastrous jargon-swamp of Word Help, which is what it automatically cuts to. Office Assistant will do a few things off its own bat if you tell it to in Preferences. But its subsequent cheery dosing of the user's eyeballs with timely Tips about using features, the mouse, and keyboard shortcuts means that to use Word without the winsome little pixie switched firmly off is to be constantly prodded in the ribs, to have your ears twisted to attention, to be told off. School will never end.

WORD PROCESSING

Sun Microsystems' Scott McNealy, responding to Microsoft's attempt to wreck the cross-platform capability of Java, claimed that they were aiming at controlling the "written and spoken language of the digital age."[9] Java's innovation was in producing a way of leapfrogging operating systems to develop a form of computing more in tune with networks than with isolated machines—something that all software bound by the desktop metaphor has yet to do. McNealy's claim conflates two forms of language, however: the formal and the natural. It rhetorically implies that the former should have access to the same rights of "freedom of speech" as the latter. Using a familiar ploy for U.S. business, Sun plays the underdog to Microsoft in what was essentially a conflict over whose version of a standard should prevail. The two forms of language are becoming increasingly close, however. The most obvious similarity is that before being compiled, code is written text, characters in a row, that is at the same time a machine. It exists both in a two-dimensional and a multidimensional processual space. This dual quality of a program feeds over into the machinery of language and suggests that both the language of Word itself and the kinds of language it machines deserve scrutiny.

Just as freedom of speech is a convenient myth under which something else entirely can safely be left to occur, the ideal of a word processor is that it creates an enunciative framework that remains the same whether what is being written is a love letter or a tax return. What kind of language is the language of Word? The nomenclature and organisational norms of Microsoft Project are already beginning to affect the way people think about business, reducing them to a stuttering sequence of Action Points, Outcomes, and milestones. Does the compulsorily informal mode of addressing co-workers that prevails in the Microsoft corporation feed over into the way it speaks to users and the way it double-guesses the way the world should begin their letters?

The templates—sample documents that users can edit to make their own, with their repertoire of "elegant fax," "contemporary fax," "formal letter," and "memo"—acknowledge that forgery is the basic form of document produced in the modern office.

The purest manifestation of this so far is 419 Fraud, named after the Nigerian statute that outlaws it. 419 consists of tens of thousands of letters, and more recently emails, apparently coming from government officials, company directors, and military officers, approaching Western bank-account holders with an incredible offer. The letters claim an insight into some impending calamity or coup and request that the recipient aid the senders by allowing their bank account to be used to move capital out of Nigeria in return for a generous commission. All that is requested is a simple down payment. And then another. A couple more. The entire operation is based around faxes and letters, an industrial-scale semiotics of fraud: letterheads, confidentiality, intimations of corrupt generals, numbers in government departments and corporate headquarters, calls to aid the world's poor, stranded bank accounts, readily available cynicism with politics, the ploy of the African simpleton working the racist sucker. The believable template, hooked up to the mailing list database, is an economic machine that works all the better, all the more profitably, if it is fuelled on fraud. There is a rhetoric of language here, but also of form. A mark is addressed in the most flattering terms, the letter-head is correspondingly well arranged. The mark for the templates is just as much the user—thinking that Microsoft will deliver the contemporary to them—as the recipient of the nicely turned-out curriculum vitae.

Whilst "in mechanised writing all human beings look the same,"[10] in the case of templates the writing itself becomes peripheral to the processing. Employment agencies on the net have been found to be advertising non-existent jobs in order to pull in trade from advertisers and the appearance of market share. Tens of thousands of people respond with their CVs. Adverts for non-existent jobs knocked up by the batchload on a CGI form are responded to by what they deserve: a multitude of self-starting no-dozers with ski-lift productivity profiles—as per the thrilling careers of the templated exemplars that come with the program.

The underlying grammar of the program conforms to that expected within the standardised proprietary interface. The menu-bar at the top of the screen provides a list of verbs that can be actioned on the nouns within the currently active window. These verbs are put matter-of-factly, as tasks: File, Edit, View, Insert, Format, Font, Tools, Table, Window, Work, Help. The same bluntness about the program's intended use can be found in the sub-programs that

direct the user to produce certain kinds of documents with the
least fuss: CV Wizard, Envelope Wizard, Letter Wizard. These are
the modes of writing it makes easy. (Suicide Note Wizard remains
uncompleted.) The Autotext toolbar already sees this easy description begin to fray, however. The writer is locked into the lexical
domain of "Dear Mom and Dad" as much as into "Dear Sir or
Madam" and "To Whom It May Concern." Mailing instructions and
"Attention" lines are offered alongside a range of closing phrases
ranging from the formal to the intimate.

To be effective, human–machine integration required that people and machines be comprehended in similar terms so that
human–machine systems could be engineered to maximise the performance of both kinds of component.[11] Word has no direct "interest" in information or communication, but rather in its facilitation.
It arranges things according to a pragmatics that is not concerned
so much with such as "When I say my mouth is open how do we
know that this is what I have said?" but with sensing and matching
every bit of such possible statements. The end point of this, of
course, is that every possible document will be ready for production by the choice of the correct template and the ticking of the
necessary thousands of variable boxes.

Michael Heim's chapter on "The Finite Framework of
Language" is particularly good in developing an understanding of
this aspect of early word processing. Jargons, metaphors, and
descriptive leaps constitute the visible language of the application—something that excites and mobilises use and exploration of
the program. The language of the program benefits from "the ambi-
guity inherent in natural language which makes possible words
both sufficiently reminiscent of past usages and semantically precise enough to indicate the new." This is not McLuhan's medial
recapitulation of past forms so much as the problem which besets
writers of Hard SF in making their scientific extrapolations of
terms and possibilities believable within currently available nomi-
native frameworks whilst still amounting to a sense of going
beyond them. For both, the prize is the same: "As the user learns
the new system, the language installs the user in the system."[12] It

is at this point that the program comes into composition with the user through the interface.

DELETE AS APPROPRIATE

In *Electronic Language,* Heim uses Heidegger's term "enframement"[13] to describe how the word processing software in effect runs a pre-emptive totalising macro on language. It is an understanding of language captured and made into a world that describes the possibilities for its use and conceptualisation on behalf of the archetypal user. However, it is an enframement that can never be pre-emptive or holistic enough, that is instead reduced to—or turned productively into—the ongoing site of conflict and transference that is the interface.

The interface is the threshold between the underlying structure of the program and the user. As a threshold it contains elements of both. The accrual of transference from the user, their incorporation, is produced in the ability to customise, through preferences, macros, autocorrections, user dictionaries, and custom templates, but also formulated in how users are conjured up as a class with needs that can be met *en masse.*

Microsoft Word was one of the first word processors for the PC with a decent graphical user interface. It made effective use of the mouse, and indeed actually often gave people a reason to buy one for the first time. However, after version 5.1 the program seems clearly to have made a break with being simply a clean, easy-to-use word processor. It became something else. The constant accrual of new tools and functions by a software bent on self-perfection means that there are no commands that will ever die in word, no function will ever be lost. The Word 5.1 toolbar is a cognitive fossil, something like a lizard brain crawled back under the stones of higher consciousness.

Not all of the interface is a disaster. You can, for example, play movies in Word with far less clutter and brushed aluminium than you can in QuickTime 4. But there is no clear sense of why you might want to do this, and if so, how that reconfigures the program and its previously core focus, writing. Whilst it is clear that writing is, under digitisation, of necessity going to be displaced, it is how this change is produced and articulated, and the clarity and interrogability of the way in which this is done, that determines whether an interface works or not. Word, of course, exists within the context of Office. Here, digital writing is not simply subsumed within an uninterrupted envelope for accessing various medial formations, but articulated, variegated, and positioned by the 419 culture of doing business.

If the behaviour of writing was solely being conditioned in this way the question of why Word's interface is the way it is would be easy to resolve. Things are also complicated by the way the software is programmed. Alan Cooper suggests that "our desktop system has so many menus and text-based dialogue boxes because all windowing systems . . . provide pre-written code modules for these functions. Conversely, none of those systems provide much pre-written code for dragging and dropping, which is why you see so little direct manipulation. A dialogue box can be constructed in six or eight lines of easy, declarative code. A drag-and-drop idiom must be constructed with about 100 lines of very intricate procedural code. The choice—for the programmer—is obvious."[14]

The economics of proprietary software constrict it so tightly that it is bound to repeat simply more of its past whilst churning out more, more faster, in order to deal with any perceived competition. For computer–human interface design as a discipline, though, the aesthetics of the interface is simply a matter of physiology applied by the spadeful. Whilst there is the minor problem of which model of human to locate as being the most relevant to the problem, there are plenty of clip-art bodies to be downloaded and used from the libraries of psychology and veterinary science. The traces of the psychometric, psychophysical, behaviourist design parameters of the human organism specified in the computer's originary conceptual infrastructure have been left behind in Word, by virtue of the sheer painful act of concentration it takes to regurgitate all that fearsome quantity of matter onto the screen.

A GREY ENVIRONMENT INCREASES EGG-PRODUCTION IN CHICKENS

The user begins to work. Everything on-screen apart from the actual contents of the focal window containing the text is lit by a continuous light from the upper left, an upper left that remains at a constant angle no matter how far you move something horizontally across the screen. Sunshine? Neon strip. This is an ultra-shallow three-dimensional world granted a pixel's width of shade to demark every separate element. When it appears, the assistant visually addresses the user as if he or she is slightly to the right and forward of where it initially appears on screen. A perspectival cross fire is under construction. The user is always, but never quite accurately, implicated as the pair of eyes that creates this by seeing. Sound feedback is used to confirm that a process has been completed, an event has occurred. Perhaps taking their cue from the promptings of the whirr and tick of keyboards and hard drives in use, Word's audio-designers have produced a series of snips, shuffles, and chimes. But whilst the program sussurates and clicks politely, its sound is always in deference to a feedback sequence that is initiated and maintained through visual interaction.

Word's graphic user interface is not simply one unremitting grey avalanche. The essential dilemma of a computer display is that "at every screen are two powerful information-processing capabilities, human and computer. Yet all communication between the two must pass through the low-resolution, narrow-band video display terminal, which chokes off fast, precise, and complex communication."[15] Microsoft's answer to this is not unique, but it is one that massively overcompensates for this bottleneck, rather than trying to develop its potential. In order to create the fastest possible route between the human and the computer, a conduit to every function must be as accessible as possible on the screen; hence many icons on many toolbars occupying much of the screen. The question is not whether this works: It clearly doesn't. Users simply remember the few icons that they use regularly and are effectively locked out of the rest of the program.

In this respect, Tufte's data–ink ratio formulation might prove useful if adapted slightly. The amount of information provided by

an interface can be costed against the number of pixels in the toolbar that it changes from the uniform background. On this reckon-
ing different toolbars begin to appear to be designed on radically
different interface conventions. Word's standard toolbar is full of
3D images, representations of real objects, globes, magnifying
glasses, cubes, and disks. There is a wide and variable use of colour
(two different magnifying glasses have different-coloured handles,
for instance) and even the graphic styles contradict one another.
(Compare the grey, two-dimensional scissors for "cut" to the multi-
coloured, three-dimensional "paste" brush.) By comparison, the
Formatting toolbar is a rather austere grey, black, and blue. The
only 3D is provided by what seems to be a highlighter pen.

There is no particular point here in assessing which style
"works," although the minimal pallette of Formatting is a little easier on the eyes in terms of peripheral vision when in use, and in
terms of reading to find or guess a particular function. Since the
icons are uniform in colour, they do not suffer from the phenomenon of brightly coloured elements (like the arrows on the "Web
Toolbar" icon or the circle on that for "Drawing") becoming visually detached from the rest of the shape. In addition to this, once
more than one toolbar is opened, "the various elements collected
together in flatland interact, creating non-information patterns and
texture simply through their combined presence."[16]

The fast conduit from human to computer becomes bottle-
necked again simply by the scale of potential interaction
sequences. A quick way to cut down on this would be to make sure
that as object-oriented program (OOP) provides a single identity for
an arbitrary set of properties and capacities, no tool appears in one
toolbar if it is already present in another. This does not solve the
problem, however. It is twofold: that of the semiotics of icons and
of the continuing spatial organisation of data in a computing environment that has gone way beyond the capacity of the desktop
metaphor to accommodate it.

Iconic languages as used in an extremely limited way in trans-
port information systems, or as proposed by the universalist
anthropology of Margaret Mead, are always doomed to fail,
swamped at best in connotation or more usually in disinterest.

Word is not, of course, alone in having too many icons. Quark XPress, for instance, has an excessive number of picture-box shapes represented on the first level of its toolbar. (One would do fine, with the rest accessible via a drop-menu.) To cope with this, icons in Word are always dependent on several kinds of textual help. Help becomes necessary solely because of the vast number of icons that are completely inexplicable.

Within the standard noun/verb grammar of the interface, icons too often look like nouns rather than triggers for verbs as functions; not only do their icons and names individually fail to cohere at an isomorphic level, their relationship to a clearer underlying system is also diminished without any payoff in flexibility or scope for developing more comprehensive—structural rather than scatter-shot—understanding.

DIGITAL ABUNDANCE

Despite the easy suspicion that the vast majority of the "features" that Word now encompasses are simply there to persuade male users that they are not doing work that was previously relegated to female secretaries, this is not to say that there is nothing worth admiring in Word. The sheer, useless inventive ugliness of the "Word Art" interface single-handedly gives the lie to the myth that allowing separate work-groups within a project to have command of what they do comes to nothing but muddle. Two dialogue-boxes' worth of minutely variable options given in fantastically unrelated swirling technicolour takes some beating. A common criticism of digital media is that it compresses time in order for more work to be extricated from the user. Word also has the capacity to dilate time, and in such corners of the program we can see the corporate imaginary of Microsoft fattening and opening up like some blushing hungry bivalve.

At the same time that the number of functions has increased, the menu bar has lengthened and the depth of choice trees has increased. In addition, as the tools become more complex, encompassing more functions, they become more abstract. That is to say that more and more of a tool's composition becomes devoted to monitoring and fine-tuning the operation of the tool. The problem (if we are to take this route) is in finding a definition of "tool." Is it a metaphor, an extension, or something that "gives visible form and physical action to a logical operation"?[17] The tool perspective in computer-interface design, as proposed by Winograd and Flores, is an endless search for a Heideggerian route to technology as a home sweet homing device. The idea runs that producing a human-centred design methodology which opposes a tool-based approach to the Death Star of Cartesianism–Taylorism allows pure form—as a manifestation of a concept or task—to be mobilised in the production of interaction design melded with thorough simplicity to the work and thought-patterns of its users. From this perspective, the radicality of Word lies instead in its absolute refusal of "Dasein"— the instantaneous being-there and fused-at-once-with-tool-and-act supposedly experienced by craftsmen, bungee jumpers, and users of the Apple Newton. The typewriter and touch-typing freed writing from the control of the eye and of consciousness. (Think of the autosave—Command-S—that most Mac users have built into them as procedural memory.) Freeing a procedure from full-frontal "consciousness" allows it to get on with things more quickly. In Word, not only can the hand not recognise the tool, but the software also makes the generous refusal of any pretence to referral to a rational outside world or any expectation of it.

"TAKE THAT BASS OUT OF YOUR VOICE; YOU TALK TO ME IN TREBLE"[18]

For Kittler,[19] Heim, and other commentators, the keyboard profoundly affects the user's access to flow. However, several more years into the phenomenon, not only has the processuality of flow been broken up into more and more granules, more features, on the one hand, but on the other, the long-term acclimatisation to word processing means that this seemingly magical release of language gained by the removal of the struggle against materials becomes normalised in comparison to its reception by these users. Flow, as in that revealed by an extended-exposure photograph of moving water, simply becomes a form, a range of potential paths already traced out.

What presents itself as a zone of plenitude is in fact an immensely complicated lock with hundreds of tumblers and latches, variations and categories. At the same time, it is too easy to allow the luxury of assuming determinism. There is no such intensity, no implicit speed or brutality to the intersection at which the user is placed by the feature-vectors of Word. Neither is there the languidity, coolness, or a sense of polysensual opening up of process. Rather there is a range of positions of balance, which is not to say of comfort, but of a neutrality, a thermodynamic flatness that always has embedded within it a number of calls to order.

The perfect text for Word is not the cut, pasted, and folded deck of samples, nor the synthesising torrent of a mind welling up into its perfect receptacle, but something like *Pride and Prejudice*. A novel sewn together by an insect plugged into a perfunctory AI and a relational database. It gathers its objects, makes lists, describes them, runs protocols, and observes their correlation with a limited variety of perceptual screens. Taking advantage of integration with Excel, the writing of realist novels could be taken to an even higher level. Once the relevant data of income, beauty, ownership of land or title, intelligence, relationship to trade or domestic skill, and familial position has been entered, the spreadsheet can run endlessly variable simulations.

Just as tools become tasks formulated around structured choices rather than material potentialities, language becomes information. What is excised from language in the mode of information is noise, what Lecercle calls the "remainder"[20]—everything that is not only the "junk" of language, its gibberish, but also what animates it.

Word combines both the receptive, control-automating mode of software typical of an automated production-line, a traffic control centre, a security system—systems designed to maintain a homeostatic, conditioned level of specific flows—and the menu-based channelling of behaviour typical of the personal computer. The discussion of the interface focussed mainly on the latter. It is how language is articulated as flow that is of concern here.

There is an argument that as texts in word processing are divisible and combinable their "contents" are eroded. "Texts are provided with a pointed structure. The argument is structured in advance and divided into separate subjects, items, and paragraphs. Items can be added or deleted later on, which may result in some loss of the course of the argument."[21] "Contents" in this sense means their relationship to truth, how closely their moral infrastructure is matched by the formal hygiene of their construction. This is an argument more around "brainstorming"[22] or idea-processing softwares such as Inspiration, where a missing or out-of-sequence cell in a flowchart can have "significant" effects, unlike word processing as exemplified in Word. But essentially, this argument is one with planned structure in writing (something contradicted by the monotonous ticking off of "issues in cyberculture" by the book which makes it—itself a waste-product of a modularised education system).

At a "lower" level than that of content, documents are also marked. It has become a commonplace that all speech acts are as much verifiable by their circumstances as by what they actually "say." At the level of import filters there is a politics of control over standards that determines whether speech can even be enacted. Open a PC Word file on a Mac and you can see where it sits on the hard disk of the author. At other times, texts produced in competing word processors or versions of Word that have "surpassed" the one you are stuck with are rendered completely unreadable. How Word interacts with and sometimes countermands the local Operating System can also produce a kind of moiré pattern of competing systems of control: Use Word on a Mac and find that if you save to the desktop the program will pedantically rearrange your files in the order of last use, no matter if you are attempting to spatially order them by a different means. Like all programs produced by Microsoft, this is the way Word is—to put it politely—optimised to work in amalgamation with their other products.

In terms of how language is inflected, Word still has some way to go before it fully automates flow or even composition. Whilst newer versions of the program are capable of assessing whether a word needs a space inserted before or after it when it is being pasted into another sequence of characters, it still does not recognise modes within language on the basis of semantics. For instance, although in AutoCorrect the first letter of a new line can be automatically capitalised, when it is cut and pasted into another section of text the capitalisation of the letter is not reversed. All that is seen is the occurrence of an event, a carriage return. The change in semantic mode is not recognised. This is, of course, what allows for the relative flexibility of use of the software and why it makes a strict division between itself and the document. Where it most visibly does not, however, is where that perfectly isomorphic machine Microsoft English is liberated from the clutches of its miserable captors, the users.

STUNT-DOUBLE FOR SPELLING

The dictionary is always a revival of language. The *Oxford English Dictionary* attempts to surpass this condition by establishing itself online, by having weather maps of linguistic norms and clusters updated second-by-second as they breed, die, and spill across the globe. (The *OED* will soon no doubt begin to become available as an online facility built into word processors as all text gradually becomes melded into one document. They would not only be able to provide exactly up-to-date corrections of meaning and spelling, but also to scan every document submitted for any savoury traces of neologism, or unlogged usage with which to update their corpus.) Even in its networked state, the dictionary can only break from its passive position of recording and instantly updating nostalgia to impose a future on language by throwing etymology into reverse, tearing the roots of words up from the mud of the past and into the speech of the present.

Fearing such a hermeneutic catastrophe, the dictionary must always remain the patient recorder of language. When it puffs its little bookshelf chest up to establish a normative function is when it loses and imposes, not its past upon the present, but its intended future of residues, already lost to language. In Microsoft Word this loser is always grappling for some purchase on any piece of text that passes it by before it is eventually swamped and drowned. This is not to say that as a knowing, personalised zombie it cannot have its uses for minor services of correction.

You have to go through several layers of interface to switch off "Grammar" and "Spelling." Where things get odder and more interesting, though, is in the user dictionary and in the setting for the personalised "AutoCorrect." User dictionaries are not repressed by the language of the dictionary in the same way that if you wear a stereo you can spend enough time in a crowded train, headbanging, farting, and beating your fingers on things or in the street yapping and gesticulating into your hands-free mobile without the constraint of the audial conditioning of your physical location. This is the same domain that an enlightened Kant allows for reason within discourses circumscribed by the securing rule of the prince rather than that of the headset. Room to manouevre. Sort of.

In order to escape this position, users incorporate the dictionary and the thesaurus into every grain of their text, running verbs, prepositions, nouns, the lot, through the mill of red and green lines. Every possible utterance becomes a combination on lookup-table results. Global English, fuelled by digitisation and a ready supply of standard components, simply becomes a permutation of all potential combinations.

User dictionaries are full of the results of skirmishes against "imperialist" English, but with only this "standard" to refer to they cut loose from conforming to a more "localised" set of rules (say, English English English) unless they have already been learned, or unless another device such as a dictionary becomes a part of the writing sequence. In this way, given no direct resource to the production of a local field of variation, they cut loose even from dialect. The divergence from the normalised language of the world is potentially immensified as these pockets of mistake, homonymy, dyslexia, take their time to inbreed and thicken their juices before lurching out into the supposedly clean white substance of language under telecommutation. One spells with correctness or a variant of it (derived from some minoritarian, dialectal, or other process of variation), or neglects to spell at all.

At the same time another private mutation is being hatched. Microsoft's recent alliance with Real Names[23] is an attempt at a rigidification of language to the point at which it becomes solely data. What is hoped by this scheme (wherein words that are also brand names typed into the search portal of Microsoft Network or the location window of Internet Explorer lead directly to the correctly denoted site) is of course that there is no longer any ground, but only a continuous and spreading act of freezing. When the meaning of a string of characters can be bought and locked into place this is the thermodynamics of language reduced to a single cryogenic chamber. For linguists a few years on there will be nothing left to study, nothing except to go round with clipboards ticking off the packets of data as they pass the test.

Other aspects of the impact of the net on Microsoft applications are readily visible within Word. The provision for some sort of HTML code-generation is clear, but there are also quite substantial beginnings of a change in use and in the construction of the user. From the beginning, Word came with a single license for a single machine. This has not changed. What has is the implication of a single author for each document. Whilst it was assumed from the beginning that several users would be authoring their own documents using the same copy of the software one after another, the massive involvement of the nets in the production of texts now produces side-effects in the construction of Word.

The economic foundation for this is the hope that by making a networked workgroup accept Word as a tool, the people who they in turn have to work with will also find it necessary in order to access the document formats or features that have become incorporated into their procedures—for instance, the layers of stages in which versions of a document can be "signed off" by managers. A slightly more straightforward way of enforcing this "usefulness" is by configuring the import filters and the formats in which files can be saved or "Sent to" in order that Word effectively works to disable its competition. Reinforcement of use is thus provided positively by features such as the ability to Track Changes and negatively by its selective ability to deal with non-native file formats.

Word demonstrably succeeds, though, in those places when it makes available the qualities of perception of data specific, at least at speed, only to computers. Where the production of a text is

spread over various authors, locations, or times, the ability to deal
with various versions—to Track Changes, for instance—allows the
computer to begin to take a part in the processing of text in a manner which maximises its own propensies without beginning to
format the user in a non-interrogable manner. The multiple and
shared versioning of documents is one level at which the nets
impact on Word. The multiple versioning of language is another,
exemplified by the incorporation of Unicode into Office 2000,
allowing the program to begin to be used more fully across a massively expanded, though not comprehensively resolved, range of
character systems. The historical genesis of computing in the West
still leaves this material–semiotic lockdown—the way in which text
is still ordered from right to left, for instance, remains one of the
most substantial legacy problems to be dealt with.

Another, perhaps more promising, way in which Word is
opened up to the net is again at a level producible only in the conjunction of computers with networks. Macro viruses such as
Melissa and the Love Bug exploit the monocultural strategy of
Microsoft, in its operating system, in its applications as a vector for
its own multiplication. Absolute standardisation, whilst infinitely
smooth in its topological isomorphism, has the quality of breeding
its own infinitely fast, massively predatory nomads. Equally, if the
strategy towards the language of the nets is really as crude as that
supposedly being put into place with Real Names, its clean world
of unambiguous meaning is inevitably going to be collapsed into
the subterranean plague-pits of language, of allegory, of puns, of a
thousand mirrored misuses.

TYPING WITH A RAISED FIST

Office's capabilities remain very much the types of applications
that defined and set the pace for the first era of personal computing. They have largely stayed in the same state but metastasised
functions. They have been impacted but not fundamentally
changed by the nets and by the multiple production of documents,
rather than retaining a singular mode of authorship. And they have
produced a sensorium that, whilst it is a near-disaster in terms of
design and overloaded with the material-semiotic infrastructure of

business, is still incapable of determining the uses to which it is put. That, at least, is some sort of usefulness.

What remains here is to ask what can be learnt from Word in terms of the production of software which moves beyond the limits of the increasingly closed models produced by an increasingly small number of corporations for a vastly increasing number of users.

Is there the possibility of producing a software which aids and encourages "autonomous work" in the terms that Gorz suggests—that is, which reiterates the process of becoming autonomous at a more profound level of producing the amalgamation which the work progresses through? Is it possible to develop software in mutuality with specific or numerous drives and tendencies that somehow maximise escape from, not always simply repurpose, the codifications of programs such as Word? At the same time, whilst autonomy is nice as a policy document, as a flag of convenience, it exists a little too much on one plane, that of work, to fully accommodate the sheer bandwidth of behaviour of life, of language. What at the very least is also needed is those moments when what we know to be true, what our certainties are about software, are lost. Is it possible to produce a software that joins with language in throwing up both moments of realisation and, for the user, devices by which it can become strange from itself?

The argument against this possibility is that software is somehow neutral. There is no need for a drive towards a reinvention of software or what is sometimes awkwardly called a "radical" software because, at bottom, all software is simply algorithms.[24] This is both compellingly optimistic, in that it refuses to get locked into determinism, but also a little more innocent than strictly necessary. Mathematics is always situated, always developed in some sort of tune with its moment in time. Ancient Greek mathematics for instance clearly developed in relation to geometry, measurement, and building. Why is there so much attention put into producing algorithms today? In order to run vast amounts of changing data through sequences of uniform and repeatable processes.

This is not to say that uses of certain forms of numerical technology are determined by inherent relations of power. It is again what they are amalgamated with that is of substantial importance. Not everything produced in Word is a CV. However, acknowledging this should not become a way of blocking processes of reinvention—particularly not as a way of slipping a more thoroughgoing conformism through as a way of seeming to, at least partially, confront the problematics of software production.

As we have seen, software is too often reduced to being simply a tool for the achievement of pre-existing, neutrally formulated tasks. Culture becomes an engineering problem.

Where this is perhaps most telling is not in the area of proprietary software, but in those areas of software production that have made an important break with it. Free, or Open Source software, particularly that available under the GNU Public License, works because it operates via one of the most useful socio-technical inventions of recent times.[25] Those active in free software are increasingly aware that it needs to develop beyond its core constituency of software written by engineers to be used by engineers.[26] This model has given us some phenomenal successes, but this process of openness needs to be opened up itself. Just as Microsoft trapped Apple into its financial domain by refusing to produce Office for their OS unless Explorer was bundled with it, proprietary software traps supposedly "free" programmers into their imaginal space by convincing them that they will have no users unless they conform to what is already known, what is already done.

The surplus rationalism that has given us tools for tasks may be free in some senses but it springs a trap upon itself every time it stays too happy to accept access to code without access to its conceptual infrastructure. Just as you can only fully reveal a phenomen if it is already disappearing, Free Software is too content with simply reverse-engineering or mimicking the cramped sensoriums of proprietary software. Copying Microsoft Word feature-by-feature and opening up the source code is not freedom. Mimesis is misery.

Whilst there is at least the beginnings of a move to collaborate with designers and other users to produce replica DTP packages, and for artists to clone Photoshop—and thus pull the practice of engineers into relation with currents it has been excluded from—there is a need to go further. Where it seems open or free approaches are most fruitful at present is in small software, making specific interventions to precise technical, economic, and social problematics. Particular bottlenecks to the distributed circulation of information are broken through, often using simple surplus rationalism as their crowbar. Despite the legal problems it encountered, the case of the open DVD player, DeCSS, is a good example of such a practice. This strategy of focussing on precise technical conflicts needs now to be intensified by drawing in antagonisms from supposedly separate fields. Geek drives to innovation must, as awkwardly and confusingly as it will happen, be coupled with the drive to make language, to cut the word up, open, and into process.

[This essay was written in parallel to work on the installation "A Song for Occupations." This piece of work took the interface of Microsoft Word apart, piece by piece, to create a visual map of its processing of language. It was first shown at the Lux Gallery in London in September 2000.]

NOTES

1. The HTML generated automatically by Word is of such low quality, full of extraneous code, that Dreamweaver 3, for instance, makes a feature of being able to automatically reformat it into useable HTML.

2. Gilles Deleuze and Félix Guattari, *A Thousand Plateaus: Capitalism and Schizophrenia,* trans. Brian Massumi (London: Athlone, 1988), p. 90.

3. For a good account of this earlier stage see "EDP Analyzer: The Experience of Word Processing," in Tom Forester, ed., *The Information Technology Revolution* (Oxford: Blackwell, 1980), pp. 232–244.

4. James Gleick, *Chasing Bugs in the Electronic Village*, http://www.around.com

5. John Hewitt, "Good Design in the Market Place: The Rise of Habitat Man," *The Oxford Art Journal*, Vol. 10, No. 2, 1987, pp. 28–42.

6. André Gorz, *Paths to Paradise—on the Liberation from Work*, trans. Malcolm Imrie (London: Pluto Press, 1985), p. 64. Gorz continues, "By its very nature autonomous behaviour cannot be explained sociologically, of course it always occurs within a socially determined field, with socially pre-given instruments. But both are reshaped in unforeseen ways to fit the requirements of a personal venture."

7. Michel Foucault, "Subjectivity and Truth," in Paul Rabinow, ed., *The Essential Works of Michel Foucault, Vol. 1: Ethics* (London: Allen Lane, 1997) p. 87.

8. Heim, op. cit., p. 10. This is a preamble to Heim's attack on McLuhan for getting wasted in the 'volcano' of the random fragmenting world. See also, Gary Genosko, *McLuhan and Baudrillard: Masters of Implosion* (London: Routledge, 1999).

9. Cited in Wendy Goldman Ruhm, *The Microsoft Files: The Secret Case Against Bill Gates* (New York: Times Business, 1998), p. 256.

10. Heidegger, cited in Michael Heim, *Electronic Language: A Philosophical Study of Word Processing* (New Haven: Yale University Press, 1987) p. 195.

11. Edwards, *The Closed World: Computers and the Politics of Discourse in Cold War America* (Cambridge, MA: MIT Press, 1996), p. 147.

12. Heim, op. cit., p. 92.

13. Martin Heidegger, *The Question Concerning Technology*, trans. William Lovitt (London: Harper Perennial, 1991).

14. Alan Coooper, *The Inmates Are Running the Asylum: Why High-Tech Products Drive Us Crazy and How to Restore the Sanity* (Indianapolis: Sams Publishing, 1999), pp. 106–107.

15. Edward Tufte, *Envisioning Information* (Cheshire, Connecticut: Graphics Press, 1990), p. 89.

16. Ibid., p. 53.

17. Malcolm McCullough, *Abstracting Craft: The Practiced Digital Hand* (Cambridge, MA: MIT Press, 1998), p. 80.

18. Reflection Eternal featuring Bahamadia, "Chaos," from Various Artists, *Soundbombing Volume Two* (New York: Rawkus Records, 1999).

19. *Discourse Networks 1800/1900,* trans. Michael Metteer with Chris Cullens (Stanford University Press, 1990).

20. Jean-Jacques Lecercle, *The Violence of Language* (London: Routledge, 1990).

21. Jan van Dijk, *The Network Society,* trans. Leontine Spoorenberg (London: Sage, 1999), p. 175.

22. Heim specifies a number of early word-processing tools (e.g. Framemaker) in which this capacity was still present.

23. http://www.microsoft.com/presspass/features/2000/03-14realnames.asp

24. For a version of this argument in linguistic terms see Joseph Stalin, *Marxism and Problems of Linguistics,* at http://www.marxists.org/reference/archive/stalin/works/1950/jun/2 0.htm/

25. See the Free Software Foundation web site at http://www.fsf.org

26. Matthew Mastracci, "Linux Office Showdown (Part 1: Applixware 5.0 M1 vs KOffice pre-beta)" at http://slashdot.org/features/00/02/22/0850251.shtml, with an excellent following thread on free word processors and office suites, including various short suggestions for a conceptual as well as technical opening-up of this area.

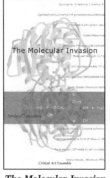

The Molecular Invasion
Critical Art Ensemble
ISBN 1-57027-138-0
140 pp $8

Having exhausted the possibilities for geographic colonial expansion, as well as reaching the fiscal limitations of virtual space, capital has invaded a new frontier—organic molecular space. CAE began mapping this development in *Flesh Machine* (1998) by examining the use of reproductive technologies and their promise for achieving an intensified degree of control over worker and citizen. *Molecular Invasion* acts as a companion to this book by mapping the politics of transgenics, and offering a model for the creation of a contestational biology, as well as providing direct interventionist tactics for the disruption of this new assault on the organic realm.

The third volume of essays in tactical media from the Critical Art Ensemble (following *The Electronic Disturbance* and *Electronic Civil Disobedience and other Unpopular Ideas*) traces the developing topographies of digital intervention. Indicating that no cultural bunker is ever fully secure, the CAE show the possibilities of trespass, unleashing semiotic shocks that collectively could negate the rising intensity of authoritarian culture. Topics include contestational robotics, the financial advantages of anti-copyright, recombinant theater-as-resistance, and the possible roles of children as tactical media participants.

"Required reading for anyone concerned with disrupting authoritarian power in all its hideous forms"—Natalie Bookchin

Digital Resistance
Critical Art Ensemble
ISBN 1-57027-119-4
165 pp $14

Read Me!
Filtered by Nettime
ISBN 1-57027-089-9
556 pp $20

Read Me! compiles writings and debates from the Nettime newsgroup and internet mailing list. This book documents the debates over emerging media technologies that are currently reshaping society. What are the liberatory potentials? Where are the points of political conflict and class struggle in this new culture? What are the pitfalls of new technology? *Read Me!* provides the beginnings of this discussion and an outline for what has become a continuing forum on the Net.

Part performative intervention, part radical polemic and activist manual, *Domain Errors! Cyberfeminist Practices* introduces a diverse international group of feminist writers, artists, theorists, and activists engaged in formulating a contestational politics for tactical cyberfeminism. This recombinant book highlights productive intersections of feminist and postcolonial discourses through critical analyses of the embodied politics of digital culture. Opening areas repressed in previous cyberfeminist discourses, the authors map contemporary social relations between women as they are mediated and transformed by digital and bio technologies.

Domain Errors!
Cyberfeminist Practices
A subRosa Project
ISBN 1-57027-141-0
288 pp $15

Dense, rigorous essays concerned not with the secret intentions lurking behind information transmission, but on the parallel worlds created through these transmissions. Media see the world as raw material for their own project, and as they are forced to constant development, the media text can never produce a final understanding. In these essays, ADILKNO looks for models of thought and magic words that will help the media text spell itself out to the point of exhaustion.

Media Archive
ADILKNO
ISBN 1-57027-079-1
224 pp $14

Open-air biological testing in New York City subways, electromagnetic mind-control, and clandestine dosing of citizens with psychotropic drugs are all part of America's little known, yet well-footnoted, history of medical abuse. *Lab USA* chronicles and illuminates these and many more events through the medium of comix. Employing declassified documents, court testimony, and interviews, *Lab USA* contrasts objective facts with powerful images to reveal the role of language and authority in the implementation of these dark deeds.

"A docucomic that reveals bad science, in the language of great art."—Sue Coe

Lab U.S.A.
Illuminated Documents
Kevin C. Pyle
ISBN 1-57027-117-8
157 pp $17.50

More Books from Autonomedia

Visit our web site at www.autonomedia.org for online ordering,
topical discussion, events listings, book specials, and more.

More Books from Autonomedia

Clipped Coins, Abused Words,Civil Government:
John Locke's Philosophy of Money   *Constantine George Caffentzis* $12

Horsexe: Essay on Transsexuality   *Catherine Millot* $14

The Daughter   *Roberta Allen* $8

Gulliver   *Michael Ryan* $8

Media Archive
   Foundation for the Advancement of Illegal Knowledge $14

Film and Politics in the Third World   *John Downing, ed.* $12

The New Enclosures   *Midnight Notes Collective* $6

God and Plastic Surgery:
Marx, Nietzsche, Freud & the Obvious   *Jeremy Barris* $12

Model Children: Inside the Republic of Red Scarves   *Paul Thorez* $12

A Day in the Life: Tales from the Lower East Side
   Alan Moore & Josh Gosniak, eds. $12

Cassette Mythos: The New Music Underground   *Robin James, ed.* $12

Enragés & Situationists: The Occupation Movement, May '68 *René Viénet* $14

Midnight Oil: Work, Energy, War, 1973–1992   *Midnight Notes Collective* $10

Gone to Croatan: Origins of North American Dropout Culture
   James Koehnline & Ron Sakolsky, eds. $14

About Face: Race in Postmodern America   *Timothy Maliqalim Simone* $14

The Arcane of Reproduction:
Housework, Prostitution, Labor & Capital   *Leopoldina Fortunati* $10

By Any Means Necessary: Outlaw Manifestos & Ephemera, 1965–70
   Peter Stansill & David Mairowitz, eds. $14

Format and Anxiety: Collected Essays on the Media   *Paul Goodman* $12

Wild Children   *David Mandl & Peter Lamborn Wilson., eds.* $5

Crimes of the Beats   *The Unbearables* $12

An Existing Better World: Notes on the Bread and Puppet Theatre
   George Dennison $14

Carnival of Chaos: On the Road with the Nomadic Festival
   Sascha Altman Dubrul $8

Dreamer of the Day: Francis Parker Yockey & the Postwar Fascist Underground
   Kevin Coogan $17

The Anarchists: A Portrait of Civilization at the End of the 19th Century
   John Henry Mackay $12

Political Essays   *Richard Kostelanetz* $14

Escape from the Nineteenth Century:
Essays on Marx, Fourier, Proudhon & Nietzsche *Peter Lamborn Wilson* $12

The Unbearables Anthology   *The Unbearables* $12

Blood & Volts: Tesla, Edison, and the Electric Chair   *Th. Metzger* $12

*Visit our web site at www.autonomedia.org for online ordering,
topical discussion, events listings, book specials, and more.*

More Books from Autonomedia

Pioneer of Inner Space: The Life of Fitz Hugh Ludlow
Donald P. Dulchinos $14

Psychedelics ReImagined *Tom Lyttle, ed.* $14

The Rotting Goddess: The Origin of the Witch in Classical Antiquity
Jacob Rabinowitz $14

The Ibogaine Story:
The Staten Island Project *Paul Di Rienzo & Dana Beal* $20

Blue Tide: The Search for Soma *Mike Jay* $14

The Blue Line *Daniel de Roulet* $12

Teach Yourself Fucking *Tuli Kupferberg* $15

Caliban & the Witch *Silvia Federici* $14

Chron!ic!Riots!pa!sm! *Fly* $10

Read Me!: ASCII Culture and the Revenge of Knowledge *Nettime* $18

Sounding Off! Music as Subversion/Resistance/Revolution
Fred Ho & Ron Sakolsky, eds $15

Against the Megamachine: Essays on Empire and its Enemies
David Watson $14

Beyond Bookchin: Preface for a Future Social Ecology *David Watson* $8

Dr. Penetralia *Th. Metzger* $8

War in the Neighborhood *Seth Tobocman* $20

Night Vision Libretto & Audio 2-CD *Fred Ho & Ruth Margraff* $20

Orgies of the Hemp Eaters *Abel Zug & Hakim Bey, eds.* $22

Forbidden Sacraments: The Shamanic Tradition in Western Civilization
Donald P. Dulchinos $14

Auroras of the Zapatistas *Midnight Notes* $14

Digital Resistance *Critical Art Ensemble* $12

Grass *Ron Mann* $20

Help Yourself! *The Unbearables* $14

Surrealist Subversions *Ron Sakolsky, ed.* $23

Work of Love *Giovanna Franca Dalla Costa* $14

Nietzsche & Anarchism *John Moore, ed.* $14

Revolutionary Writing *Werner Bonefeld, ed.* $15

Communists Like Us *Félix Guattari and Antonio Negri* $8

Bolo'Bolo *p.m.* $8

Autonomedia
PO Box 568
Williamsburgh Station
Brooklyn, NY 11211-0568
T/F 718-963-2603
info@autonomedia.org

*Visit our web site at www.autonomedia.org for online ordering,
topical discussion, events listings, book specials, and more.*